CW00971379

MiG-3 Aces
of World War 2

SERIES EDITOR: TONY HOLMES

OSPREY AIRCRAFT OF THE ACES • 102

MiG-3 Aces of World War 2

Dmitriy Khazanov and Aleksander Medved

OSPREY
PUBLISHING

Front Cover
The first Luftwaffe air raid against Moscow was launched during the evening of Monday, 21 July 1941, and it consisted of 195 bombers – Ju 88s from KGs 3 and 54, He 111s from KGs 53, 55, 28, III./KG 26 and KGr.100 and Do 17s from KGs 2 and 3 – concentrated against the Soviet capital. No fewer than 170 communist fighters were scrambled to intercept the raiders, and one of the latter fell to Soviet test pilot Capt Mark Gallay. His victim was a Do 17 from 9./KG 3, flown by Leutnant Kurt Kuhn. Gallay was serving with the 2nd Separate Fighter Air Squadron of the Moscow Air Defence Forces at this time, the unit having been hurriedly established and manned by test pilots from the Flight Testing Institute of the Peoples' Commissariat of Aviation Industry.

A test pilot from 1937, Gallay made ten sorties in MiG-3s from July to September 1941, although the 9./KG 3 machine was his only success during this period. He gave the following detailed account of this engagement in his memoirs;

'I clearly saw the angular stumps of the aircraft's wings, engines and two-fin tail. It was a Dornier 215 or possibly a 217, and I was flying straight into it – my MiG shook slightly when it passed through the bomber's slipstream. Crosses, crosses on the wings. Immediately, as if by instinct, I fired a long burst at the crosses. This was the wrong thing to do, for the Dornier was still about 400 m away. I removed my finger from the trigger. Then, as I got closer, I started firing at the cockpit and engines. It seemed that I had hit the bomber. Suddenly, lines of return fire from both the upper and lower gunners' stations stretched out towards my fighter. I still do not know how they did not shoot me down. I managed to escape, and continued my pursuit. I made my second approach from slightly below so that the upper gunner could not aim at me. I fired a short burst at the cockpit and starboard engine and quickly slipped off to the side so that any return fire missed me.

'I made several more approaches like that, aiming my guns at the bomber's fuselage and engines. The return fire also stopped. I fired and fired, but the bomber kept on flying. One last approach, followed by a long burst, and suddenly the Dornier jerked oddly off to the right in a banking turn. It seemed to hang in mid-air in this position for a few seconds, before the angle of bank increased sharply and the bomber dropped out of the searchlights and crashed a few seconds later' (*Cover artwork by Mark Postlethwaite*)

First published in Great Britain in 2012 by Osprey Publishing
Midland House, West Way, Botley, Oxford, OX2 0PH
44-02 23rd Street, Suite 219, Long Island City, NY, 11101, USA

E-mail; info@ospreypublishing.com

Osprey Publishing is part of the Osprey Group

A CIP catalogue record for this book is available from the British Library

ISBN: 978 1 84908 442 0
e-book ISBN: 978 1 84908 443 7

Edited by Bruce Hales-Dutton and Tony Holmes
Page design by Tony Truscott
Cover Artwork by Mark Postlethwaite
Aircraft Profiles by Andrey Yurgenson
Index by Michael Forder
Originated by United Graphics Pte Ltd
Printed and bound in China through Bookbuilders

12 13 14 15 16   10 9 8 7 6 5 4 3 2 1

Osprey Publishing is supporting the Woodland Trust, the UK's leading woodland conservation charity by funding the dedication of trees.

www.ospreypublishing.com

CONTENTS

CHAPTER ONE
DEVELOPMENT AND DEPLOYMENT 6

CHAPTER TWO
BAPTISM OF FIRE 16

CHAPTER THREE
GAINING EXPERIENCE 28

CHAPTER FOUR
THE DEFENCE OF LENINGRAD 38

CHAPTER FIVE
HEROES OF MOSCOW 58

CHAPTER SIX
NAVAL MiGS 74

APPENDICES 88
COLOUR PLATES COMMENTARY 92
INDEX 95

DEVELOPMENT AND DEPLOYMENT

The defeat of the Republicans in the Spanish Civil War highlighted deficiencies in the quality of aircraft, particularly fighters, supplied by the USSR. The Soviet political leadership was quick to recognise this, and Supreme Commander-in-Chief Joseph Stalin convened a meeting in February 1939 to consider the country's aircraft industry, and its products. A further meeting, in May, was attended by many of the leading aircraft designers, engineers and manufacturers' representatives. The result was a call for a new generation of fighters, together with new engines to power them. Many design teams were involved.

The most promising efforts were expected from Nikolay Polikarpov and his design bureau. Polikarpov had developed the I-15bis biplane and I-16 monoplane, which now constituted virtually the entire fighter inventory of the VVS RKKA (*Voenno-Vozdushnye Sily Raboche Krestiyanskoy Krasnoy Armii* – Air Force of the Workers' and Peasants' Red Army). In 1939 its latest product, the I-153, was the first, and indeed only, biplane fighter to go into production with a retractable landing gear. A major effort went into producing the I-180 monoplane, which was intended to replace the I-16. The project was undermined by a fatal crash that killed test pilot Valery Chkalov, however.

In 1939 the first liquid-cooled AM-35 engine was assembled and bench-tested at Moscow's Aircraft Factory No 24. The new powerplant demonstrated an ability to develop 1350 hp for take-off and 1250 hp at an altitude of 4500 m (14,600 ft). To maximise output Aleksander Mikulin's design bureau progressed to the more powerful AM-37 variant with 1400 hp for take-off. When Mikulin's engineers confirmed the powerplant's expected performance characteristics, Mikhail Kaganovich, the Peoples' Commissariat of the Aviation Industry (*Narodniy Kommissariat Aviatsionnoy Promishlennosti*, NKAP), suggested that Nikolay Polikarpov should use the AM-37 in his latest fighter designs. The engine did indeed appear promising, and Polikarpov duly chose it for his I-200 project.

The signing of the non-aggression pact between the Soviet Union and Germany signalled warmer relations between the two countries. Many Soviet aircraft

Nikolay Polikarpov receives an award from the Chairman of the Presidium of the USSR Supreme Soviet, M I Kalinin

designers and engineers, including Polikarpov, visited Germany to see the aircraft factories there and inspect the Luftwaffe's frontline equipment. While Polikarpov was away, some major changes were made to the personnel in his design bureau. The NKAP appointed Artyom Mikoyan, younger brother of VKP(b) Political Bureau member Anastas Mikoyan, to take charge of the Polikarpov Design Bureau. Artyom Mikoyan had previously been a military representative at Factory No 1. A few months earlier, in March 1939, he had joined the Polikarpov bureau as a team manager, before becoming the I-153 project supervisor in charge of production.

The I-200 project was presented in Polikarpov's absence, N I Adrianov, N Z Matyuk, V A Romodin and M I Gurevich, who then headed the bureau's project department, acting as spokesmen for the new aircraft.

By the end of 1939 the NKAP leaders had decided that an independent project team should be established within the design bureau. A I Mikoyan was appointed to lead the team responsible for developing the new high-speed fighter and putting it into production. The team was strengthened by the appointment of the knowledgeable and erudite Mikhail Gurevich as Mikoyan's deputy.

The creators of the I-200 fighter (designated MiG-1 and then MiG-3 in production), Artyom Mikoyan (left) and Mikhail Gurevich

From the start the I-200 project was given the highest priority, and development proceeded rapidly. By the end of 1939 the VVS RKKA had approved the mock-up, and the designers progressed to the production of engineering drawings. As work on the AM-37 engine had not yet been completed, the less powerful AM-35A was used instead. To speed up the project even further, additional personnel were recruited. The enlarged staff worked ten to twelve hours a day, seven days a week. The introduction of the loft templating method of blueprinting also helped the team, whose draftsmen now only had to create 2500 sheets of original drawings. This in turn meant that the blueprints were completed by 10 February 1940.

The I-200's airframe was of a mixed wood and metal construction, with the forward part of the fuselage – including the engine mountings – consisting essentially of a welded tubular framework. The remaining

The fuselage of the prototype MiG was manufactured by gluing several layers of plywood sheets onto a special template, with further strengthening of the resulting shell provided by several frames

fuselage section was a wooden monocoque. The cockpit was covered by a one-piece Plexiglas canopy, but it lacked armoured glass in the windscreen. The wing was a single-spar type, with the metal centre section employing the Clarke YN profile. Two self-sealing fuel tanks were installed between the primary and secondary spars. A third would be added later to the fuselage ahead of the cockpit. The outer wing panels were made of wood.

In its 'basic' form the fighter was armed with a large-calibre BS machine gun and two ShKAS rifle-calibre weapons mounted in the nose and synchronised to fire

through the propeller disc. The fighter could also carry two bombs (up to 200 kg in weight) or six RS-82 rocket projectiles mounted in underwing racks. The fighter could also carry two bombs (up to 200 kg in weight) or six RS-82 rockets mounted on underwing racks. RSI-3 radios were installed in every third airframe, with receivers in the others.

Mikoyan and Gurevich paid great attention to the construction of the I-200 airframe so that it could be built as a series of separate sub-assemblies. Removable outer wings and fuselage sections, together with the single-strut undercarriage units and simplified retraction mechanisms, could be constructed separately. They would then be brought together for final assembly, thus making efficient use of Factory No 1's production capacity. At the same time, pre-assembly manufacturing processes were also simplified through the use of casting and drop-stamping technologies, placing the I-200 far ahead of other Soviet aircraft of the time in respect to the efficiency of its manufacture.

The first I-200 prototype had its oil radiator on the left-hand side of the engine. The oil temperature control shutter was positioned within the air intake on this machine, but on production aircraft the shutter was repositioned aft of the intake. The prototype also lacked armament and radio equipment

An early-production MiG-3 fitted with RS-82 rocket projectiles during testing at the aviation armament range

The cockpit canopy of the I-200 prototype opened to the right-hand side via a hinge, while production aircraft featured a more traditional sliding canopy. The I-200's single-piece undercarriage doors were mounted on the gear legs, but this was later changed to a two-piece design

Wind-tunnel tests performed at the Central Aero and Hydrodynamics Institute (*Tsentralniy Aero-Gydrodinamicheskiy Institut*, TsAGI) confirmed the correctness of preliminary design calculations. As a result, on 4 March 1940, the Council of Peoples' Commissars (*Soviet Narodnykh Comissarov*, SNK) ordered the first three I-200 prototypes, which were expected to reach a maximum speed of at least 640 km/h (400 mph) at 7000 m (22,750 ft). But Mikoyan and the director of Factory No 1, P V Dementyev, decided not to limit themselves to three airframes and instead built five prototypes. Four would be for flight-testing purposes and the fifth for further static tests at TsAGI.

The first airworthy prototype was completed and prepared for factory flight-testing by 31 March 1940. Anatoly Brunov was appointed engineer in charge, with Arkady Ekatov (Factory No 1's senior aviator) acting as the leading test pilot. The maiden flight was made on 5 April, and it was followed by a series of tests that demonstrated the fighter's close compliance with the design specifications both in the air and on take-off and landing. These findings were promptly reported to Aleksey Shakhurin, the new NKAP Commissariat, who had succeeded Kaganovich in January.

An important milestone was the test aircraft's participation in the May Day military parade. Ekatov swept over Red Square at high speed and stunned the Soviet leaders, particularly VVS RKKA and industry chiefs. On 24 May the required top speed of 648.5 km/h (405 mph) at 6900 m (22,450 ft) was attained and reported. The response of the national leadership was both immediate and predictable. The following day the State Defence Committee approved the new fighter for production under a specially issued order. On the 31st, before completion of the factory test programme, to say nothing of the State acceptance trials, the NKAP Commissariat officially announced that the I-200 would be produced at Factory No 1 under the designation MiG-1.

I G Rabkin, one of the most experienced engineers at the Scientific Research Institute of the Air Force (*Nauchno-Issledovatelskiy Institut Voenno-Vozdushnikh Sil*, NII VVS) had this to say about the striking

A MiG-3 in the large wind tunnel at the TsAGI

difference between the I-153 *Chaika* biplane, which had now been phased out of production, and the new I-200;

'The I-153 and the I-200 represented two distinct eras in the development of the Soviet aircraft industry – the biplane on the verge of extinction and the first of the new generation of monoplane fighters. The former, with its struts and bracing wires and other sources of drag, the latter, smooth and aerodynamically clean, with its finely polished skin which replaced the old fabric covering.'

To initiate production of the new fighter, however, designers, engineers and test pilots had to overcome formidable difficulties. There were the inevitable teething troubles, but the MiG-1 proved to be tricky to fly, with a propensity to spin easily. The AM-35A engine was also demonstrably the product of hasty development,

The first production MiG-3 sits on the ramp at the TsAGI facility at Kacha between range determination tests in February-March 1941

and there were plenty of 'bugs' to cause further problems. In late 1940 and early 1941 three fatal crashes were reported, one of which, on 13 March, killed Arkady Ekatov.

Nevertheless, the defects were gradually eliminated and the production rate steadily increased. But as VVS RKKA commanders wanted the fighter's operational range to be doubled to 1000 km (625 miles), the new MiG-3 version, featuring an additional fuel tank, was promptly developed and introduced into production. Data from the Soviet archives suggest that in the first quarter of 1941 50 MiG-1s and 283 MiG-3s were delivered to the Moscow military district and units on the Soviet Union's western borders.

DEPLOYMENT

As fighter pilots began an intensive training programme, the new aircraft were being distributed more or less evenly between the fighter regiments, making it difficult to determine which was the first to re-equip with the MiG. Military representatives at Factory No 1, however, reported that regular westward shipments began during the second half of January. On the 21st, for example, 35 MiG-1s were transported by rail to 41st Fighter Air Regiment (*Istrebitelniy Aviapolk*, IAP) at Belostok. Ten days later, ten fighters were shipped to the Kacha Flying School in the Crimea via the seaport of Evpatoria. On 25 January 31 MiGs were sent by rail to Kaunas for 31st IAP. A few days later two trains, each loaded with 35 MiG-3s, departed for Lvov (28th IAP) and Kacha (41st IAP).

It was initially suggested that 41st IAP would receive MiG-1s for operational service testing purposes, and that the MiG-3s would go to 146th IAP stationed nearby. Factory No 1 organised special teams to accompany the shipments, assemble the fighters on-site and remedy any defects. In late January, a team of NII VVS specialists headed by Snr Lt A G Kubyshkin was sent to Lvov to train senior officers of 28th IAP. The team included the third most senior military engineer, V I Alekseenko, and a number of other specialists. Their first task was to hand over technical manuals and operating instructions for the MiG-1 and AM-35A engine.

As pilots in the field familiarised themselves with their new equipment they suffered a number of accidents, some of them due to airfields whose surfaces were still muddy after the winter. On 3 March Snr Lt Evgeny Gorbatyuk damaged his fighter while landing on the bumpy field. He would eventually become an ace and Hero of the Soviet Union, claiming seven kills while flying MiGs. Flights were briefly suspended, but the work undertaken by the NII VVS team helped 28th IAP pilots complete their conversion training by 15 March. By that time the 17 leading pilots had flown 59 training sorties. Many commanders, including 28th IAP's CO, Col A P Osadchiy, his deputy, Capt I V Krupenin, and deputy divisional commander, Lt Col L G Kuldin, received praise for their skill.

The Air Force of the Moscow Military District also received a significant number of new MiG fighters, and by early April 16th and 34th IAPs were able to begin preparations for the May Day parade. Mindful of the event's political significance, 34th IAP CO Maj L G Rybkin detailed his 20 best pilots and engineers to visit Factory No 1 for a ten-day study of the aircraft. Here, they received exhaustive training on how to fly and maintain the MiG-3. Among the first pilots to master the new fighter were M G Trunov, A V Smirnov, V M Naydenko, N G Scherbina and A F Lukyanov.

A month earlier, on 10 March, the first two MiG-3s had landed at Vnukovo airfield, near Moscow, for 24th Fighter Air Division (*Istrebitelnaya Aviadiviziya*, IAD) CO, Col I D Klimov, and his training inspector, Maj D L Kalarsh. Soon there were enough aircraft available for most of the pilots to begin their training, and the first to complete the course was regimental CO L G Rybkin. A veteran of the Winter War with Finland and holder of the Order of the Red Banner, Rybkin demanded the best of his subordinates at all times, but he was always prepared to help them master the new aircraft, and particularly its low-speed behaviour.

The story of the pilots' conversion training would be incomplete without a short description of an incident reported on 10 April in the Baltic region. On that day an unidentified aircraft crossed the border and flew deep into Soviet territory. A standby flight of MiG-3s from 31st IAP, 8th Combined Air Division (*Smeshannaya Aviadiviziya*, SAD) took off from one of the airfields at Kaunas to intercept the intruder. Only Jr Lt Akimov returned from that sortie, Lt Aksyutin bailing out and Jr Lt Evtushenko perishing when his fighter crashed.

The findings of the subsequent investigation suggest that Akimov followed the intruder up to an altitude of 11,000 m (35,750 ft) and then stalled into a spin after attempting a shallow zoom. Having recovered from the spin into a dive, Akimov pulled his control column back too sharply and blacked out from the resulting g-load. He was able to recover and bring his fighter home. The nearest approach to the twin-engined aircraft was reported by Aksyutin, who got close enough to make out the German crosses on its fuselage and wings and the swastika on the tail. Moments later Aksyutin also pulled his control column back too sharply, and unable to recover from the ensuing spin, he took to his parachute.

Military engineer Andrey Kochetkov, who rushed to Kaunas to conduct the investigation, pointed out that all the pilots had made the same error in taking their fighters beyond critical angles of attack while performing sudden low-speed manoeuvres at high altitude. He also found that the young pilots lacked theoretical knowledge of the MiG-3. Another unwelcome finding was that Evtushenko had never previously flown the MiG-3, and had only made 13 flights in the MiG-1, all of which had been training circuits over the airfield. He had never flown above 5000 m (19,500 ft). On that last fatal sortie, Evtushenko's aircraft had been at 9500 m (30,875 ft) when it entered the spin. The pilot had managed to recover into a dive at about 1000 m (3250 ft) but failed to pull out, and his aircraft had hit the ground. Evtushenko had probably lost consciousness due to excessive g-loads.

Despite this incident, conversion to the MiG-3 proved to be easier than with contemporary fighter designs from LaGG and Yakovlev. On 27 May 1941 VVS RKKA headquarters chief Gen P F Zhigarev reported to Stalin that multiple defects had been uncovered in newly delivered LaGG-3 fighters. Only one of the 14 air regiments to be re-equipped with them had by then actually completed the conversion training and re-equipment programme. Pilot feedback suggested that the LaGG-3 was

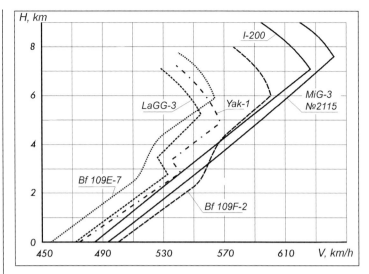

H, km — V, km/h

I-200 / LaGG-3 / Yak-1 / MiG-3 №2115 / Bf 109E-7 / Bf 109F-2

Speed and altitude characteristics of fighters participating in combat on the Soviet-German front in the summer of 1941. As this chart clearly shows, the new crop of inline-engined Soviet monoplane fighters (the MiG-3 in particular) were built for high-altitude combat

The underwing Berezin BK 12.7 mm machine gun mounting was fitted to a number of aircraft produced by Factory No 1 from September 1941

much easier to fly than the MiG-3. On the other hand, more unresolved manufacturing defects and design shortcomings had been encountered in the fighters from Lavochkin, Gorbunov and Gudkov (LaGG) than in the Mikoyan and Gurevich product. As a result, Zhigarev proposed that some of the fighter regiments still awaiting deliveries of the LaGG-3 or the delayed Yak-1 should instead be re-equipped with the MiG-3.

As more pilots mastered the new generation high-speed fighters, the MiG-3 proved it could easily dive to 500 km/h (312 mph) and beyond, and then trade speed for altitude by zooming up to 600-700 m (1950-2275 ft). This was expected to give MiG pilots a valuable advantage in combat. The Bf 109Es initially fielded by the Luftwaffe in the northern and southern sectors of the frontline after the German invasion of June 1941 demonstrated poorer vertical manoeuvrability and could not follow the MiGs in zooms and turns – nor for that matter could the I-16.

Before the war some of the most experienced and perceptive pilots argued that the introduction of the new fighter would require the development of new tactical manoeuvres, as the I-200 was initially intended to be a high-altitude fighter. Back in 1939 many aviation strategists had believed that most aerial combats would be fought at higher altitudes. As a result, the AM-35A engine, which developed its maximum power within the 5000-8000 m (16,250-26,000 ft) range, was considered suitable for the new fighter.

Similarly, the MiG's lack of manoeuvrability and wider banking turns at lower and medium altitudes, together with its excessive landing speed, could be overlooked. These minor deficiencies would be more than compensated for by the aircraft's superiority at higher altitudes, however. The realities of Soviet-German air combat would soon dispel such beliefs.

Re-equipment of the western military districts with the new aircraft continued in May when 20 were delivered to 4th IAP near Kishinev and 55th IAP in Beltsy. That same month the NII VVS ordered Lt Col P M Stefanovsky to 20th SAD to facilitate the conversion training of pilots from these two regiments, which were part of the division. Petr Stefanovsky subsequently recalled;

'The division had two complete sets of fighter equipment comprising the outdated I-16 and I-153 and the brand new MiG-3, but by the time I arrived they wouldn't dare even to make a test flight with the latter type, so I had to push it. Surprisingly, the pilots weren't at all enthusiastic about the new aircraft, and nobody volunteered to master it. Well, I had to show off right away with the MiG-3. So I took off and squeezed everything I could out of the aircraft, and a bit more. Once I landed it appeared that their suspicious attitude towards the fighter had gone. The pilots were cured of the fear of the new machine. The ensuing conversion training had to be completed in some haste as time was pressing, and we flew from dawn to dusk.

'I don't know how that air division subsequently performed during the war, but during the opening phase its freshly retrained pilots flew their MiG-3s with exceptional skill and outstanding courage.'

Snr Lt Aleksander Pokryshkin was one of Stefanovsky's trainees during May and June. He would go on to become a celebrated ace on the MiG-3, receive three stars as a Hero of the Soviet Union and eventually be promoted to the rank of air marshal. Pokryshkin wrote in his memoirs about those days;

'On 22 June my regiment faced the enemy with the MiG-3, the new fighter that required many new skills and a major effort to get the best out of it. As for me, I fell for the aircraft at once. It was like a mettlesome racehorse. Handled by a forceful rider it would go like an arrow, but if you lost control it would smash you with its hooves. Designers rarely achieve a perfect balance between an aircraft's flight performance and its ability as a gun platform. In any design there are always some problems to be found.'

Pokryshkin agreed with Stefanovsky's opinion that the successful combat deployment of the new fighter required more flying practice and additional courage. That meant trainee pilots putting aside their natural fears and pushing the aircraft to its limits in respect to stresses and g-loads, just as if they were engaging the enemy. Pokryshkin said;

'I liked aerobatic flying and performing at the limits of speed and altitude. I always did my best to fly aerobatic manoeuvres so that I could instinctively coordinate the movement of my hands and feet with those of the control surfaces, especially when pulling up into a vertical manoeuvre or recovering from a dive. In my enthusiasm, I outperformed my comrades, who erroneously believed that actual air combat would be like our mock battles over the airfield. They tended to be too mechanistic, carrying out their training in a way that assumed that our strict formations would never break up and scatter.'

The forthcoming war would soon shatter many established beliefs, including the strict adherence to the air combat tactics that had dominated the pre-war doctrine. It would also mean both a shift of priorities in fighter pilot training and a review of the strengths and weaknesses of Soviet combat aircraft. As Pokryshkin noted;

'In every new fighter of that era we saw new achievements in engineering. But many of the MiG-3's advantages were obscured by the few disadvantages that were initially apparent. The aircraft would only reveal its secrets to those pilots who spent enough time practicing and learning how to take advantage of the opportunities it offered.'

Aleksander Pokryshkin's prewar unit, 55th IAP, was certainly not short of expert pilots. However, they all had to complete their conversion to the new type before they could perform to the best of their abilities. Because of the tensions on the western borders, many commanders increased the tempo of training. The first pilot from the regiment to complete his training on the MiG-3 at Pyrlitsa airfield, in the Prut River valley, was Jr Lt V I Figichev, a future Hero of the Soviet Union and one of the most successful aces on the southern front. He would score nine aerial victories, downing eight German and one Rumanian aircraft during his first month in combat over Moldavia and south Ukraine.

Figichev's baptism of fire came on 9 June 1941, 13 days prior to the German invasion. Sighting an intruding Ju 88, he approached the Junkers bomber and tried to force the pilot to land at an advanced airfield on the Soviet side of the border. The intruder, with German crosses clearly visible on its wings, immediately turned back towards Rumanian territory. The flight of MiGs followed the Ju 88 and penetrated several kilometres into Rumanian airspace. The resulting diplomatic incident involving a hostile Rumanian government might have resulted in Figichev's arrest had it not been forgotten upon the outbreak of war.

As the conflict approached, the situation on the Soviet Union's western frontier became even more tense. Together with the air regiments previously mentioned, six other units had been almost completely re-equipped with MiG-1/3s by the outbreak of hostilities. These were 15th IAP at Kaunas (8th SAD, led by Col V A Gushchin); 124th IAP at Belostok, 126th IAP at Dolubowo and 129th IAP at Tarnovo (all three units were controlled by 9th SAD, led by Maj Gen S A Chernykh); 23rd IAP at Lvov (15th SAD, led by Maj Gen A A Demidov); and 149th IAP at Chernovtsy (64th IAD, led by Col A P Osadchy).

As at 21 June 1941, units deployed in the Baltic, Western, Kiev and Odessa military districts had a total of 753 MiG-1/3s available to them, including 80 undergoing maintenance. In addition to this force, 300 MiGs were deployed as interceptors by regiments within the Moscow and Leningrad Air Defence Forces.

The MiG-3's streamlined, aerodynamically clean shape was admired by many of the Soviet pilots who converted to it from I-153 and I-16 fighters. A typical response from early 1941, when the first examples began to reach frontline units, was this quote from 16th IAP's Technician Varenik. 'The MiG aircraft were standing menacing, long-nosed. The pilots, mechanics and air fitters surrounded them on all sides, touching wings, looking into the cockpits, searching to find where the armament was installed, examining the undercarriage. The new aircraft were interesting to everyone'

BAPTISM OF FIRE

As with other Soviet aviation units deployed near the country's western borders on 22 June 1941, the fighter regiments equipped with MiG-1/3s suffered heavy losses during the first days of the war. Most of the Luftwaffe's initial attacks targeted the advanced airfields where the newest Soviet aircraft were based.

Of the 4426 fighters deployed at the five western military districts nearest to the border on 22 June, 917 were MiGs. But there were only 234 MiGs, out of 1821 surviving fighters, still intact two days later. These figures did not, however, include data from the Odessa Military District, later known as the southern front, where about 150 MiG-3s were deployed. Many of the 99 brand-new fighters that had been ferried to Orsha in the Western Military District in the early hours of the war were also probably lost, but they were not included in the reports. The conclusion, therefore, must be that the MiGs suffered the highest losses of any fighter type both in percentage and absolute terms.

On 22 June the situation along the whole border area prevented the Soviet pilots from using their skills and taking advantage of the strengths of their fighters. There was an almost complete absence of anti-aircraft artillery coverage at the airfields, many of which were still under construction and full of field engineers and local workers. The aircraft were parked in rows and not camouflaged, offering perfect targets for the enemy. Lines of communication were cut during the early stages of the invasion and enemy pilots scored direct hits on fuel storage tanks. To make matters worse, there was a shortage of ammunition and spare parts. And as it was a Sunday many pilots and groundcrew were off duty or away on leave.

The gravest losses were suffered by 9th SAD. It had a strength of 37 MiG-1s and 196 (other sources say 200) MiG-3s at the time of the German invasion. The entire inventory was destroyed and the division had virtually ceased to exist by 25 June. The divisional commander, S A Chernykh, a Hero

The result of a German air raid on a Soviet airfield. Caught lined up in the open on the morning of 22 June 1941, these MiGs would clearly never fly again

of the Soviet Union, was promptly court martialled and sentenced to death. The division's few surviving documents suggest that 9th SAD's pilots claimed to have shot down 85 enemy aircraft near Ostrow Mazowiecka, Zambrow, Lomza and Bialystok (now in Poland) on 22 June. According to German loss reports and accounts from individual Soviet regiments, this figure was exaggerated by at least a factor of ten.

129th IAP CO, V P Rulin, recalled the general feeling of expectation as the last days and hours of peace ticked away;

'Among the high-ranking commanders, the feelings of nervousness steadily increased. The Western Special Military District's intelligence reports became ever more alarming. We witnessed daily incursions by Luftwaffe aircraft, and when they were intercepted they never complied with our orders or signals. Moreover, their behaviour became daily more impertinent.'

While nobody expected an attack so soon, pilots of 129th IAP were among the few who were ready to meet enemy raiders early on the morning of 22 June. At dawn 12 MiG-3s and 18 I-153s took off from Tarnovo to intercept the intruders, and by 0405 hrs they had engaged a dozen Bf 109s. MiG-3 pilot Snr Political Instructor A M Sokolov claimed his first aerial victory. Another successful interception resulted in 18 He 111s being turned away from Tarnovo airfield. Their crews released their bombs haphazardly and retreated, but the enemy persisted, raids continuing as Luftwaffe aircraft dropped small splinter bombs. By 1000 hrs a series of attacks by small formations of Ju 88s and Bf 109s had destroyed 27 MiG-3s, 11 I-153 *Chaikas* and eight training aircraft on the ground at Tarnovo. They had also rendered the airfield inoperable.

In the absence of any communication with headquarters, Col Y M Berkal, who had become regimental CO a few days earlier, ordered a series of redeployments, initially to Kwatery, then to Zabludovo and finally to Dobzhenevka. In the war's first two days 129th IAP reported that its pilots had flown 125 sorties – most of them in MiG fighters – on patrols along the border in an effort to protect their airfield, as well as on redeployment. While feeling comparatively at ease in the air, the Soviet fighter pilots found themselves exposed to German bombing raids while on the ground. This was due to the lack of anti-aircraft defences and also to the exact knowledge of the Soviet airfields' locations displayed by enemy raiders. It appears that 129th IAP's last five MiG-3s were destroyed at Baranovichi airfield on 24 June.

Some of the advanced Soviet airfields were sited close to the border – Tarnovo, for example, was only 12 km (7.5 miles) inside Soviet territory. The intensive training flights, including those by MiG fighters, during May and June 1941 had made the task of pinpointing the airfields' locations an easy one for the Germans. In several cases Soviet airfields had been deliberately shelled by German artillery and even bombarded by mortar fire in the opening hours of the invasion. Such attacks severely damaged air

A 122nd IAP fighter heads out on a combat sortie in the summer of 1941. The absence of an aerial indicates that the fighter lacks radio equipment

17

MiG pilots from an unidentified unit await the order to scramble. The aircraft's prominant radio mast is clearly visible

compressors, and their tanks, at these sites. The resulting lack of high-pressure air had deprived units of the means to start aircraft engines. This in turn meant that groundcrews were forced to destroy perfectly serviceable MiGs so as to prevent them being captured intact by rapidly advancing enemy troops.

In addition to the destruction of equipment there were grievous personnel losses too. Of the 248 pilots available on 22 June, only 170 reported to Orel a week later to receive new aircraft and assignments. Reports of the first day's fighting indicated the number of combat losses. Jr Lt N F Erchenko was killed in an air battle near Tarnovo airfield, while Jr Lt A A Radugin was not even able to take-off. He was burned to death in the cockpit of his MiG-3 at Dobzhenevka airfield. Several pilots reported shrapnel wounds during the German air raids, but most were listed simply as 'failed to redeploy'.

During the first two days of fighting 129th IAP pilots had expended almost 50 complete loads of ammunition for their MiGs – about 15,000 12.7 mm and 36,000 7.62 mm rounds – without encountering any failures. Yet neighbouring 124th IAP reported repeated failures with the armament of its new fighters. In one incident in June the failure of a 12.7 mm gun's synchronising mechanism resulted in a propeller blade being shot off, followed by an emergency landing.

The reports of armament failure resulted in on-site repairs, but they failed to prevent further problems. On 22 June Jr Lt D V Kokorev reported that his machine guns had jammed after he had fired only a few rounds at the invading enemy at 0430 hrs. He then resorted to ramming what he later stated was a Do 215, which he downed after destroying its tail with the propeller blades of his MiG-3. The Soviet pilot was able to return to his home airfield. German reports suggest that Kokorev's victim had in fact been Bf 110 Wk-Nr. 3767 of II./SKG 210, which had been lost near Zambrow. This may well have been the first ramming attack on the Eastern Front.

Kokorev's regiment was deployed at Wysokie Mazowieckie, 40 km (25 miles) from the border. Compared to other 9th SAD bases, this was a relatively small airfield. Nevertheless, 70 MiG-3s were deployed there, together with 29 I-16 fighters. Such numbers restricted ground manoeuvring and limited the new fighter's advantages. It should also be noted that the MiGs, unlike more nimble predecessors like the I-153 *Chaika*, required runways 500-600 m (540-650 yrd) long and the ability to make unobstructed take-offs and landings.

At another 9th SAD unit (41st IAP) nine MiG-3 fighters survived through to 23 June, only to meet their fate the next morning. Four days later VVS RKKA CO Gen P F Zhigarev ordered 12 brand-new MiG-3s to be delivered to the regiment. By then, however, 9th SAD had been disbanded and 41st IAP attached to 43rd IAD. During the subsequent air defence of Mogilev, MiG-3 pilots Snr Lts P I Zabelin, D G Korovchenko, A A Lipilin, P A Tikhomirov and I D Chulkov distinguished themselves.

In addition to 41st IAP, the remaining nine MiG-3 fighters of 162nd IAP also participated in these battles after being deployed to Baranovichi on 23 June under the command of Lt Col Reznik. 43rd IAD would soon be left without any MiG fighters at all, while 41st IAP would be attached to 23rd SAD to continue operations at the western front until 7 July. The last delivery, made in June, comprised 18 MiG-3s that arrived at 170th IAP, attached to 47th SAD.

Hero of the Soviet Union Snr Lt A A Lipilin of 41st IAP. By October 1941 he had flown 112 sorties and claimed eight and three shared victories, as well as numerous targets destroyed on the ground. Flying on the northwest front, Lipilin survived the war

EARLY SUCCESSES

Many Soviet commanders reported that the MiG-3's combat deployment during the first days of the war had been successful. On 30 June, for example, General Headquarters representatives Marshals K E Voroshilov and V M Shaposhnikov wired a message to the Council of Peoples' Commissars stating;

'It is necessary to deliver the maximum possible number of bombers, ground attack aircraft and fighters. The latter have proved to be more effective than their German counterparts. We have only 11 MiGs left, and those are busy all day long, being the most powerful weapon we have to oppose the Germans. Today, 29 June, two of our MiGs engaged a flight of Messerschmitts and shot down three of them.'

The special-purpose regiments of test pilots played a notable role during the first phase of operations against the Luftwaffe. The establishment of these units had been initiated by Hero of the Soviet Union S R Suprun, who had personally commanded 401st Special Purpose IAP (IAP ON). 402nd IAP ON was placed under the command of another experienced pilot, Lt Col P M Stefanovsky. The two regiments were equipped with 67 MiG-3s of the latest type and departed for the western front on 30 June.

Well-known Soviet test pilot Mark Gallay, who worked at the Flight Research Institute and was to become a prominent author, participated in the MiG-3 interception missions over Moscow during the summer of 1941. He commented on the success of that initiative as follows;

MiG-3 pilot Grigorenko (first name and unit unknown) was credited with shooting down three enemy aircraft in the summer of 1941

Snr Lt A G Kubyshkin of 401st IAP ON prepares for take-off. Credited with five and six shared victories, he flew 70 combat sorties in the MiG-3

'We test pilots had logged many more flying hours on the new fighters, including the MiGs, than any of the regular service pilots. It was just a case of bad luck bringing some good luck. The saga of the engine problems and other teething troubles experienced by Soviet high-speed aircraft led to our impressive flying experience and thorough knowledge of the fighters' behaviour, thus allowing us to feel at home in their cockpits.'

On the other hand, Mark Gallay admitted some of the obvious shortcomings in the mobilisation of test pilots from the NII VVS and aircraft factories. These included a lack of combat and night flying experience, as well as limited aerobatic skills. These deficiencies were also present in frontline units too, afflicting both commanders and their pilots. This in turn had a significant impact on the outcome of the aerial battles fought during the opening stages of the war, for most of the commissioned pilots had had insufficient time to complete their MiG-3 training. Apart from recent flying school graduates, these men had previously performed confidently with earlier fighter types, but Gallay highlighted the general lack of experience with the MiG-3 in a combat environment. 'In essence, we found ourselves unable to perform all those little tricks that are the basic elements of an actual air battle'.

The first combats also revealed further equipment defects. After 25-30 hours in service, the cockpit canopies would become spattered with oil from oil tank breather vents. Armament and electrical system failures were reported time and again. And the cost of throwing into battle test pilots lacking air combat experience was frequently too high. Moreover, as aerial engagements usually happened at low altitudes, even the best Soviet aces could not take advantage of the MiG-3's strengths compared with its main adversary, the Bf 109F. Casualties during the first days included Stepan Suprun (killed on 4 July), who was the first fighter pilot to be nominated for a second Hero of the Soviet Union accolade.

Men like Lt Col Konstantin Kokkinaki (401st IAP ON CO following Suprun's death) and Maj V I Khomyakov were among the most effective MiG-3 pilots. So too was Snr Lt Aleksey Kubyshkin, later to become a prominent test pilot, who proved to be both skilful and courageous. He was also the unchallenged master of low-altitude aerobatics with the MiG-3, his speciality being steep turns at full load. In two months at the front, Kubyshkin flew 70 combat sorties, participated in 32 aerial

engagements and, according to the authors' sources, scored two individual and four shared victories.

The first night flight from an advanced airfield not equipped for nocturnal operations was probably that performed on 6 July by Snr Lt Afanasy Proshakov. Having sighted an enemy aircraft flying overhead, Proshakov immediately took off, stalked the intruder and shot it down with his first burst. German documents suggest that his victim was night reconnaissance Do 17P Wk-Nr. 3572 of 3(F)/*Nacht* wing, which was reported missing with three crew while on a mission to the towns of Polotsk and Sebezh – Idritsa airfield was located mid-way between them. Although the bomber's return fire punctured the MiG's fuel tank, Proshakov was able to glide home and land safely, using his landing light for guidance.

Developments on the northwestern front, and the part played by the MiG fighters in the opening battles there, can, to some extent, be judged by the political summary of the first two days of military operations from one of the Red Army formations involved. While paying tribute to the pilots' courage, Brigade commissar Ryabchy noted;

'Among the flight officers, many believe that the enemy aircraft are superior to our SB medium bomber and I-16 and I-153 fighters. Not enough of the newer types of aircraft are available. Moreover, the pilots have not completely mastered the new machines that are available. Most of the pilots have not completed their combat training and have never participated in exercises and could not be expected to take full advantage of their equipment in their first experience of air combat.

'The first combat sorties have revealed shortcomings with the MiG-3. The fighter's engine requires new sparking plugs every three flying hours, and when operated from dusty fields the radiator core becomes clogged with dust, resulting in engine overheating. A serious shortage of oxygen prevents pilots from reaching critical altitudes, reserves for wartime operations having not been sufficiently built up due to a limited number of oxygen bottles available. Furthermore, there are only three compressor stations to service 24 air regiments. There are not enough sparking plugs for the entire complement of MiG-3s either. When the war started only 700 spare plugs were available, which was clearly not enough to sustain continuous operations.'

The commissar's emphasis on the lack of supplies and equipment for regular high-altitude flights appears to have been something of a diversion from the root cause of the problem, as German aircraft never flew above the 1200-2000 m (3900-6500 ft) envelope. On the other hand, the particular reference to MiG-3s rather than to other aircraft types in that and other reports of the time suggests the high level of activity by the new fighters in the first few days of the war.

On the northwestern front, two air regiments of 8th SAD (15th and 31st IAPs) entered the fray after they had been almost completely re-equipped with MiG-1/3s. Both units had high reputations. Established in the mid-1930s, 15th IAP was, in fact, the direct successor to the famous 3rd corps fighter air wing of the Russian Imperial Army, which had its origins in June 1914. In the winter of 1939-40, the regiment went into action against the Finns, and some veterans had fought in the Spanish Civil War and Mongolian border clashes with Japan. While it

This factory-fresh MiG-3 has been fitted with underwing canisters, which could in turn be filled with small bombs

might appear unlikely that such experienced pilots would encounter major problems with new equipment, the documents suggest that even they had difficulties, resulting in fatal accidents.

31st IAP was among the few units to survive the first wave of Luftwaffe attacks on Soviet airfields. Immediately before the war, the regiment's squadrons had been dispersed – the 3rd squadron (comprising 13 MiG-3s and 18 I-16s) stayed at Kaunas, while three other squadrons (39 MiG-1/3s and two I-16s) were redeployed to Karmelava, 13 km (eight miles) northeast of Kaunas. But after intensive pre-war training flights, almost half of the MiGs – 24 fighters – were in need of repair, and either had to be abandoned or destroyed in the face of the advancing German invaders.

Pilots from an unidentified MiG unit discuss air combat tactics before a sortie

As for 15th IAP, it suffered severe losses at Mitawa airfield. More than 180 aircraft were there on the evening of 22 June, including the entire MiG-3 complement of 7th SAD's 10th IAP – its pilots had just received the new fighters and started their training. The extent of 15th IAP's material losses remains unclear, but 8th SAD reported a total of 75 new fighters destroyed on the ground during the initial days of the invasion, probably including the 40 MiGs of 15th IAP.

Reports dating back to June 1941 contain frequent references to several pilots who had performed particularly creditably. In 31st IAP they included regimental CO Maj P I Putivko, who was seriously wounded in an air battle, Capt B V Ovechkin and Lt S S Smyslov. Reports from 15th IAP single out Snr Lts A A Dmitiriev, P T Tarasov (who scored six individual victories with the MiG-3) and A D Shemyakov. Among those lost in the uneven battles were Capt I A Dobzhenko, Capt N Boyarshinov and Lt I I Schultz.

These heroes of the first days of the conflict had to repeatedly engage the Luftwaffe because of the acute shortage of pilots trained to fly the MiG-3. In 15th IAP for example, just 23 pilots had been taught to use the new fighter by 22 June. Additional flights in the Baltic region were halted upon the outbreak of war, leaving some pilots lacking sufficient training to allow them to fill the gaps in their ranks caused by casualties.

To preserve the combat experience accumulated by the survivors of the early days, commanders in the northwestern front air force concentrated the pilots of 8th SAD that were able to fly the MiG-3 within 31st IAP. The unit was redeployed to Karamyshevo airfield to defend Pskov against enemy air raids. Some documents suggest, however, that 15th IAP was also redeployed to that area and continued flying MiGs.

On the northwestern front MiG-3-equipped units lost their combat-ready status later than those on the western front. On 12 July 15th IAP was withdrawn to the rear to be reformed, and two days later a similar decision was taken in respect of 31st IAP. The latter unit's reports indicate that, during the initial phase of the war, its pilots flew 714 combat sorties, fought in 34 air combats and claimed 13 aerial victories. The cost, however, was high. The regiment lost all 63 MiGs that it had on its strength on 22 June, as well as seven that had arrived as reinforcements, plus a number of I-16s. History records that the regiment's casualties during this period included 13 pilots killed in air battles and 11 others reported missing. However, when 31st IAP's surviving pilots and ground staff were paraded in Moscow on 17 July before receiving new MiG-3s, the personnel losses were revealed as more serious, as indicated in the table below;

31st IAP Personnel

Date	Pilots	Technicians	Airmen	Others	Total
22 June 1941	91	60	113	12	266
17 July 1941	21	48	100	12	181

In the southern sector of the Soviet-German frontline, the German *Luftflotte* 4, which opposed the Kiev Special Military District air force, met the fiercest resistance and suffered the highest losses among the invaders. Updated Luftwaffe sources note that KG 51 lost 15 Ju 88s and listed 52 aircrew as missing on 22 June alone. At least three of the bombers were reported shot down near Lvov, matching data submitted by the Soviet air defence staff and 15th SAD. The latter's documentation suggests that MiG pilots of the division's 23rd and 28th IAPs claimed to have shot down three Ju 88s.

23rd IAP was based at Adamy airfield, 80 km (50 miles) northwest of Lvov, on 22 June. Ten MiG-3s that had been at readiness were scrambled, while 29 more were held on the ground. These aircraft were damaged in seven subsequent German air raids, leaving 13 fighters out

A MiG-3 taxies in following the completion of yet another combat mission. During the summer of 1941 VVS RKKA fighters were often more at risk from German attack when on the ground between sorties than when in the air

Lt Victor Bashkirov, who later became one of 122nd IAP's most successful pilots with 15 individual and two shared victories to his credit, poses with his MiG-3 in late 1941. Bashkirov was awarded the title of Hero of the Soviet Union in February 1944, by which time he was flying the Yak-9

of action. By the evening of the 22nd, regimental CO Col A I Sidorenko reported that only 19 MiG-3s remained intact. Despite the losses, the unit's pilots flew 124 combat sorties and reported 12 battles between opposing formations, with three victories claimed that day.

Lt Col Cherkasov, 28th IAP's CO, had taken his duty elements away from Chunev airfield in the Lvov complex before the German attack. Afterwards, one air group intercepted enemy bombers near Rava-Ruska, while another patrolled Lvov. The unit's pilots would report completing 114 combat sorties, and the destruction of four enemy aircraft, by the end of the day. Archive documents state that 'some pilots flew up to eight or even ten combat sorties that day'. Ironically, most of the regiment's losses were caused by Soviet flak, which shot down three MiG-3s. By the end of the day 28th IAP was down to its last 19 serviceable aircraft.

Before the war 11 pilots from 23rd IAP had become the first regular VVS RKKA pilots to fly the MiG-3 at night. Nocturnal patrols were therefore undertaken immediately the war started. These came to an abrupt halt on 23 June when Snr Lt Polupanov collided with another MiG whilst landing. Polupanov was killed and both fighters destroyed. No further nocturnal sorties were reported.

As well as interception missions, the MiG pilots performed a number of other tasks, including reconnaissance of enemy troop positions, protection of aerial assembly areas and repelling raids on base airfields. By the end of June 1941, 23rd and 28th IAP had claimed 35 German aircraft and one autogiro destroyed between them. Most of these victories were credited to MiG pilots. On the other side of the coin, the regiments had a combined strength of just 19 serviceable fighters by 1 July.

MiG pilots were among the most successful Soviet aviators on the southwestern front. 28th IAP – and probably the entire 15th SAD – opened its combat score with the Bf 109F shot down by Lt N B Timokhin near Lvov on 22 June. Two victories were later claimed by his squadronmate Jr Lt A M Murashko, who continued flying even after being twice wounded. On 24 June Snr Lt Gladyshev of 23rd IAP destroyed a bomber near Zubov airfield before he was himself shot down and killed. His victim was a Ju 88 misreported as an He 111. On the 25th Lt G F Monastyrsky of 28th IAP was attacked by three

Messerschmitts while on a solo reconnaissance mission. He survived to claim two victories upon returning to his airfield.

While praising Gen A A Demidov's 15th SAD aces for their airmanship, reports from the high command reproached many pilots for air combat tactics that were too defensive. Pilots of 149th IAP (64th SAD) were judged to be less successful MiG-3 operators. That observation was not particularly surprising, for the unit had received its new equipment too late for its pilots to master the fighter prior to the outbreak of war. Moreover, on 22 June the unit had lost 21 MiGs in a bombing raid on Chernovtsy airfield.

Even so, German sources reported a loss on 22 June due to what was described as a 'long-nosed, high-speed Russian fighter of a new type'. This was a clear description of the MiG-3, which could only have been operated by 149th IAP. Having targeted an airfield near Stanislaw, a formation of six Ju 88s from 9./KG 51 were heading back for the border when one fell behind due to problems with its left engine. An element of three Soviet fighters appeared and the pilots were probably so surprised to encounter such easy prey that they hesitated in shooting it down.

The German crew's chances of survival were slim, and the gunner and the wireless operator desperately fired back. One of the MiGs dropped out of the battle with its engine smoking. The two remaining fighters continued the pursuit, setting the enemy bomber on fire with several bursts. Ju 88A-5 Wk-Nr. 8259 crashed near the town of Stryi, 60 km (37.5 miles) south of Lvov. The four crewmen bailed out, the pilot and navigator landing amid Soviet troops and being posted as missing. The gunner and the radio operator evaded capture and crossed back into German-held territory to be picked up by a patrol from the Wehrmacht's 52nd Army Corps.

It was on the southern front where MiG-3 units had their biggest impact on the contest for the control of the skies. In south Ukraine, Moldavia and Bessarabia, the VVS RKKA presence was as intense as it was elsewhere along the frontline, but there it ensured the Soviets' numerical superiority over the opposing German *IV. Fliegerkorps*. The availability of Rumanian air force units could not change the situation in any tangible way due to their pilots' lack of combat experience and equipment with mainly obsolete aircraft.

The German and the Rumanian units were unable to suppress the Soviet air defences and airfields along the southern segment of the frontline as they did elsewhere. This was because the Axis offensive was not as intensive here as in other areas. Nevertheless, on the morning of 22 June numerous attempts to destroy as many aircraft on the ground as possible were reported. The key targets were the airfields on which the newest Soviet aircraft were based. As early as 0515 hrs pilots of 55th IAP were called upon to intercept 20 He 111s, escorted by 18 Bf 109s, heading for Beltsy airfield. The timely warning by ground observation posts enabled regimental commander Col V P Ivanov to give the eight MiG-3 interceptors standing at readiness the order to take-off. Even so, three new fighters and a small fuel storage tank were burnt out.

After the first few days of fighting the losses suffered by MiG-3 fighters in combat and due to accidents reported by 4th and 55th IAPs were less severe than those sustained by other wings deployed near the border. Of

Ubiquitous GAZ-AA trucks were often used to transport pilots to their airfield, these aviators hailing from a MiG-3 unit

the 122 (regimental documents say 115) new fighters accepted by 20th SAD on the eve of war, 82 MiGs, including 70 serviceable fighters, had survived by 26 June and were available for operational use by 53 pilots. Having more or less effectively countered the initial raids, the pilots of these units soon began attacking Wehrmacht troops and their vehicles. On 23 June Su-2 and SB bombers entered the fray, escorted by MiG-3s. The next day it was reported that the newest fighters had flown 79 combat sorties.

Of the MiG-equipped regiments, 4th IAP's combat performance in late June appears to have been the most successful. Regimental CO Maj Victor Orlov was the first to master the MiG-3, and also the first to open his personal victory score. At 0715 hrs on 22 June he shot down a Bristol Blenheim displaying Rumanian markings and the tactical number '38'. It crashed near Kishinev airfield, killing all three crew, including the commander, Capt Vasilesku. At about midday on the 23rd, squadron commander Capt Afanasy Karmanov (a former Moscow aircraft factory test pilot) shot down two Bf 109s in a major engagement. Both pilots took to their parachutes and were eventually captured.

German reports suggest that they were flying Bf 109Es belonging to II./JG 77, which had been heading for Grigoropol airfield to attack aircraft based there. The loss of Feldwebel Hans Illner's fighter was, however, incorrectly attributed to flak. Such misreporting was common to both sides in the conflict. But further doubt results from the absence of a report about the second of Orlov's victories because German reporting of losses was usually very thorough. It is likely, therefore, that the enemy pilot was wounded and taken to a hospital in territory soon to fall to the invaders, enabling the pilot to return to his unit. Documents from the Peoples' Commissariat of Internal Affairs indicate that such a case was reported, but they do not name the pilot concerned.

The MiG-3's combat debut on the southern front was also marked by the unnecessary loss of pilots and equipment. 20th SAD's Regimental Commissar Melshakov pointed out that many MiG-3 losses were due to armament failures caused by faulty synchronising mechanisms, overheating of the barrels of ShKAS machine guns, defects in BS guns and other minor problems. 20th SAD's CO, Gen A S Osipenko, also highlighted the negative role played by tactical flaws. Having reviewed operational reports from the war's first week, he pointed out instances of poor or missing camouflage, too formal mission statements, poor formation keeping, particularly on return flights, and other similar deficiencies.

Due to the hurried preparations for war, training programmes failed to address the issue of communication within formations, as well as fighting tactics. As a result, there was no wingman to cover Capt Afanasy

Karmanov's tail while he was chasing a German fighter, and his MiG-3 was shot down by future ace Oberleutnant Kurt Lasse of 9./JG 77. Karmanov tried to bail out but his parachute failed to open. Having shot down two enemy aircraft earlier that same day, he was posthumously awarded the title of Hero of the Soviet Union.

In a review of reports from 146th IAP of 21st SAD (Odessa Military District), two trends become evident. Firstly, the Soviet fighter pilots frequently reported shooting down Hurricanes, Savoias and PZLs rather than the expected

A MiG-3's armament (two 7.62 mm ShKAS machine guns and a solitary Berezin 12.7 mm weapon) are checked before a sortie. Note that the armourer on the left is standing on a pad that he has placed on the fighter's wing so as to protect it from scuffing

Heinkels, Junkers and Messerschmitts because of the Rumanian Air Force presence in that area. This was also why, on the morning of 25 June, a 'Breguet XIX' was reported as having been downed by a MiG-3 pilot west of Falesti. It was more likely to have been an IAR-39 reconnaissance aircraft on a leaflet-dropping mission.

Secondly, most aerial victories were reported as being shared by several pilots. On 24 June, for example, the destruction of four SM.79s is attributed in Soviet documents to Jr Lt A M Zharin's flight, and the following day a Ju 88 to the element led by Capt O Farafonov. On the other hand, the night victory of 146th IAP deputy squadron commander Snr Lt K P Oborin on 25 June was reported as an individual score. Two of his comrades, who had taken off in company with another MiG-3 and an I-16 from Tarutino airfield near Odessa, failed to locate a pair of enemy bombers reported by observers on the ground. However, at 0320 hrs, Oborin made a lone attack on an He 111 and, having expended his ammunition, finally downed the German bomber by ramming it.

Despite bent propeller blades and a damaged spinner, to say nothing of several bullet holes, Oborin was able to land his fighter at his base airfield by the lights of a truck. After that, the name of the pilot who had made the first nocturnal ramming attack of the Great Patriotic War was immortalised, and Oborin was immediately recommended for a decoration. He would, however, not live to receive it because of fatal wounds sustained on 18 August.

German documents state that Oborin hit and damaged He 111H Wk-Nr. 6830, which managed to make an emergency landing near Odessa. The other Heinkel, belonging to 4./KG 27, landed nearby to rescue the crew.

After that and other similar incidents, 146th IAP CO Maj K D Orlov strongly recommended that Soviet fighters should attack the well-armed and armoured He 111 bombers 'in pairs or, preferably, flights, and thus increase the chances of victory and reduce the risk of being shot down by concentrated return fire'. But the main conclusions about the various aspects of the MiG-3 combat employment still remained to be drawn.

GAINING EXPERIENCE

In the summer of 1941 the most crucial sector of the war between the Soviet Union and Germany was the western front, where the Luftwaffe had concentrated its main striking force. These formations included II and VIII *Fliegerkorps* of the powerful *Luftflotte* 2. It was in that area that the VVS RKKA reported suffering the worst losses, leaving the surviving pilots to battle with overwhelming numbers of enemy aircraft. In an attempt to change the situation, the Red Army ordered the best reserve units to join the fray. The newly arrived pilots were immediately thrown into the struggle for control of the sky over the battlefield, replacing the units that had been decimated by the onslaught and which were now being withdrawn for replenishment.

Soviet reports suggest that in July 1941 the USSR's aviation units at the front were mainly equipped with obsolete aircraft (such as SB medium bombers and I-153 and I-16 fighters) drawn from reserves. The overall picture was further aggravated by the acute shortage of fighters, particularly modern machines like the MiG-3.

Situation reports indicate that between 6 and 12 July MiG-3 pilots flew 97 combat sorties and lost seven fighters in aerial engagements. Total losses during the same reporting period included 32 MiGs. This meant that every third sortie resulted in a fighter lost. MiG-3 losses reported by the Western Front Air Force within a single week of July 1941 were as follows;

Date	Losses in air combat	Losses to anti-aircraft fire	Missing	Destroyed on the ground	Non-combat losses	Total
6 July	3	-	2	2	-	7
7 July	2	9	1	-	1	13
8 July	1	-	1	-	-	2
9 July	-	-	7	1	-	8
10 July	-	-	-	-	-	-
11 July	1	-	-	-	-	1
12 July	-	-	-	1	-	1
Total:	7	9	11	4	1	32

It was, however, too early to lose heart, and the Soviet commanders were able to bring up formidable aircraft reserves during the last week of July. One result was that 122nd IAP, equipped with 32 MiG-3s, was transferred to the Reserve Army Front Air Force and attached to the air group commanded by Col Zotov. After the first three days of fighting, the regiment had lost all of its I-16s and been withdrawn to the rear from Lida. The pilots and the unit commander, Col A P Nikolaev, completed an expedited conversion course at Ryazan Air Navigation School. This consisted of just eight solo MiG-3 flights per pilot, but the training was reported to have been successfully completed due to the high level of competence exhibited by the pilots involved. Despite the haste only two minor accidents were reported. All three squadron COs, Maj V V Puzeykin, Capt A F Semenov and Snr Lt F A Orlov, had seen combat in the minor conflicts that had broken out before the German invasion.

From the start the MiG was able to demonstrate its fighting capability when operated by well-trained and experienced pilots. On 24 July Orlov left Yershi airfield to investigate reports of a concentration of German motorised troops near the town of Belyy. On the way he encountered a flight of Ju 88s, which he attacked. In the high-speed engagement that ensued three bombers were shot down. However, according to regimental reports, the MiG-3 then 'turned back eastwards, flying at slow speed and trailing grey smoke'. An infantry commander confirmed the triple victory, and recommended that 'the heroic pilot should be decorated'. Orlov failed to return to Yershi and was posted as missing.

German data suggest that the Soviet pilot had intercepted reconnaissance aircraft operated by 4.(F)/14 that were heading eastwards at 5000 m (16,250 ft). The reports also acknowledge the loss of a pair of Ju 88Ds. The third aircraft was probably damaged, but its pilot managed to bring it home. Captured German NCO Rudolph Wagner revealed that the flight's objective had been to reconnoitre the roads north of Smolensk. They had been the last three aircraft of the original nine that the unit had had on strength at the start of the war in the east, the crews being ordered to fly in close formation at a higher altitude than normal so as to ensure their safety. Despite their compliance with this requirement, one Soviet MiG-3 had proven to be enough to surprise the trio and bring their mission to a premature conclusion.

Few sorties ended with such success for Soviet pilots in 1941, however. On 26 July, for example, six MiG-3s led by 122nd IAP commander, and Hero of the Soviet Union, Aleksander Semenov failed to protect six Pe-2 bombers of 410th Bomber Air Regiment (*Bombardirovochniy Aviapolk,* BAP). All were lost, together with a MiG. One of the Pe-2s was later found to have crash-landed in Soviet-held territory. Subsequent investigation found that a veteran fighter pilot by the name of Shagov was to blame

This MiG-3 required major repair after being force-landed with battle damage

for the losses. He was branded a coward, having left his comrades and wingmen unprotected when he fled the scene. In accordance with normal Soviet practice at that stage of the war, Shagov was court-martialled.

Material held in the archives of JG 51 is more revealing. It suggests at 1900 hrs on 26 July two elements of Bf 109s had shot down six Pe-2s within five minutes, and that an I-18 (the initial German designation for the MiG-3) was shot down about 15 minutes later. Four fighters from 9./JG 51 engaged the escorts, while two more pairs from 4./JG 51 attacked the bombers in a pincer movement. The two groups exchanged roles to complete the destruction. Leutnant Maximilian Mayerl and Feldwebel Otto Schultz reported two victories each. Clearly, the German aces were more skillful than their Soviet counterparts, and that appears to have been the main reason for their success.

This incident was far from being the only case of a single MiG-3 pilot being held personally responsible for a collective failure. Six days earlier Lt Aleksander Gorgalyuk, a member of a MiG squadron attached to 47th SAD, was ordered to take off from Shaykovka airfield, eight kilometres (five miles) south of Spas-Demensk, to intercept a flight of enemy bombers that had just appeared on the horizon. As his fighter was not ready when the bombs started exploding on the airfield, Gorgalyuk hid in some bushes rather than risk being killed while taking-off.

The following day he damaged his MiG-3 on landing, and the two incidents were seen as grounds for criminal prosecution. The court martial sentenced Gorgalyuk to death, but he was given a stay of execution to prove himself in battle. After flying a number of successful missions and scoring six individual victories, plus two shared, the conviction was removed from his personal record in October 1941. By that time Gorgalyuk had been transferred to 180th IAP. He was later awarded the title of Hero of the Soviet Union.

129th IAP followed 122nd IAP to the war zone, where it was attached to 47th SAD. The regiment had also been moved up to the front after a brief period of replenishment and conversion training. Unlike their 122nd IAP counterparts, many 129th IAP pilots had become familiar with the MiG-3 before the war, and were therefore able to act as instructors to their less experienced comrades. At the same time they were able to continue intercepting enemy bombers and reconnaissance aircraft threatening Orel. Between 22 July and 8 August the regiment flew 483 combat sorties from Shaykovka airfield, reporting participation in 20 aerial engagements and claiming seven victories. The most successful pilot was squadron commander Aleksey Panov, who claimed a Bf 109 and a Bf 110, as well as a Fi 156 Storch liaison aircraft that had made a rather unexpected appearance over the frontline.

The new Soviet fighters could, however, have been much more effectively employed, but the few MiGs were thinly spread across many locations and commands, and not all the units operating them were well organised or led. Following several weeks of intense action, many hitherto unaddressed design and manufacturing defects were also uncovered. At the same time the interaction between different units and between air and land forces remained largely uncoordinated. All these factors hindered the effective utilisation of the few combat-ready regiments that were then available. The result was many unnecessary losses.

A MiG-3 prepares for an attack on advancing enemy troops, the aircraft having been fitted with RS-82 unguided rocket projectiles on its underwing racks. Initially, aircraft were made rocket compatible by groundcrew in the field, but from October 1941 Factory No 1 began installing wing rails on new MiG-3s as they progressed along the production line

A MiG-3 patrols its home airfield to provide cover for other aircraft taking off and landing

Western Front Air Forces lost 16 MiG-3 in air combats, plus a further ten to flak during July. Another 38 were reported as missing during operational sorties, although ten of those had made emergency landings and were later recovered, while nine more had been destroyed on the ground and three MiGs lost in crash landings. On the other hand, no fatal accidents involving MiG-3s were reported, and the rate of losses to causes other than combat was as low as 4.5 per cent. This might have been attributable to the high standard of pre-war pilot training.

Air force staff at several levels were eventually able to accumulate enough combat performance data to reveal certain positive and negative aspects of the new equipment. The following shortcomings were identified in the MiG-3 – short radius of action, excessive landing speed resulting in crashes at short and bumpy advanced airfields, frequent failure of the wing-mounted machine guns, unbalanced propellers and failures of the gun synchronising mechanism, leading to punctured propeller blades. Wing-mounted guns were quickly removed from aircraft operating on the western front because they were considered unnecessary. Also reported were malfunctioning pneumatic systems caused by insufficient pressure, which resulted in the machine guns jamming, failure of the main landing gear locking mechanism and failure of tail wheels to extend. Finally, tyres were found to be too sensitive to field conditions, with too many replacements being required.

It was also reported that some MiG pilots seldom flew with their cockpit canopies closed, despite the drag and resulting loss of speed. They explained the habit was due to the lack of an emergency jettisoning mechanism and the need to improve forward vision over the long nose, despite the potential for being covered in oil splashes. Rearward vision was also severely obscured by the high fuselage fairing protruding above the low-set cockpit. In addition, pilots reported that the MiG-3's cockpit was poorly ventilated, leading to discomfort in hot summer weather.

While many of the reported defects were well known, some were new. For example, operations from dusty airfields caused a reduction in engine life by up to 30 flying hours due to radiators and cooling system pipes becoming clogged with dust, and the resulting overheating increasing wear of cylinders and pistons. And the lack of interchangeable landing gear doors, water-cooling pipes and outer wing panels in fighters built since the start of the war hindered repairs, especially on examples delivered to emergency landing sites.

The lack of tactical training for Soviet pilots also had an adverse affect on the MiG-3's combat effectiveness. There was a clear example of this on the southwestern front when a flight of Bf 110s made a bombing and strafing attack on Zubov airfield, where 23rd and 28th IAPs were deployed. They were able to evade pursuing MiGs by making a simple steep turn followed by diving down and hugging the ground to escape.

'Defensive circle' tactics adopted by Luftwaffe crews when under attack also seemed unfamiliar to the Soviet pilots. This was highlighted by 15th SAD CO Gen A A Demidov, who noted that German aircraft 'form a circular chain'. Having analysed the the defensive tactic of forming a circle so that each aircraft in the chain could protect the tail of the one in front, Demidov stated 'That sort of formation enables them to protect each other in a very reliable way. I therefore believe we should also adopt this useful tactic'.

Also noteworthy is 15th SAD CO's request for more MiGs, submitted to southwestern front air force commander Gen F A Astakhov. He stated that his division's regiments needed 'at least 10 to 15 serviceable MiG-3 fighters because our aircraft are close to the end of their service lives'. During the summer of 1941 it was the practice to operate aircraft on rotation, but the implication of Astakhov's request was that the few surviving MiG-3s were not being maintained because of a shortage of spare parts. Dozens of fighters were out of action and, because they could not be withdrawn from the combat zone, represented easy prey for the enemy. In July, therefore, the southwestern front's air force was down to 15 to 30 fighters, which in pre-war days would have barely been enough to equip two squadrons. The southwestern front air force subsequently received reinforcements from the southern front air force.

MiG-3 availability in the southwestern front air force was as follows (serviceable/unserviceable aircraft);

An observer scans the sky before the order is given to remove the camouflage netting from the fighters parked behind him in preparation for take-off

Division	11 July 1941	17 July 1941	29 July 1941
15th SAD	8/2	11/2	1/-
16th SAD	2/1	-	-/2
36th IAD	-	-	8/3
64th IAD	-	4/3	8/7
Total MiG-3 fleet	10/3	15/5	17/12

Total complement of combat-ready aircraft			
	249/131	296/137	278/141

Fighter regiments like 23rd IAP had to be withdrawn to be reformed and replenished. 28th IAP also temporarily stopped using the new fighters in combat, its last eight MiGs being transferred to 36th IAD of the Kiev area defence force, which was covering the city itself plus the bridge over the River Dnepr and the local railway junction. It was not until 2 August that 28th IAP's pilots received 12 new MiG-3s. Ferried in by senior political instructor A V Rudenko and Lt V F Petrov, they enabled the pilots to resume operations with their favourite fighters under the command of Maj N F Demidov. At the same time, the high-altitude, high-speed interceptors proved effective in the air defence of Kiev in contrast to the Polikarpov fighters that were not fast enough to engage the Ju 88s.

Southwestern front air force archives provide an interesting analysis of the strengths and weaknesses of the MiG-3 by 15th SAD equipment engineer Maj Bagdasaryan. In accordance with normal Soviet practice of the time, his report emphasised the shortcomings. In this case they included faulty installation of the large-calibre machine gun, which highlighted play in the mounting pivots, loose cables in the reloading system of the underwing guns and faults in gunsights that were proving vulnerable to oil spattering. Bagdasaryan's most interesting conclusion was that the underwing machine guns should be retained, despite their negative impact on the fighter's speed and manoeuvrability. He said;

'The MiG-3's five-gun armament configuration is preferable. It gives the pilots greater confidence in air combat, enabling them to rely both on the large-calibre guns as the primary weapon and the ShKAS guns as the secondary one. What they need is a good optical gunsight or, at least, an extra ring sight.'

By August, 15th SAD had 52 fighters available, 36 of which were serviceable. On the 6th of that same month, 19th Bomber Air Division (*Bombardirovochnaya Aviadiviziya*, BAD) had deployed west of Kiev. It had been tasked with operating alongside 15th SAD, and on the first day of joint operations (7 August) reported flying 78 sorties. To improve integration and effectiveness, one fighter squadron of seven serviceable MiG-3s was directly subordinated to 19th BAD CO, Lt Col A K Bogorodetsky. Unfortunately, 7 August also saw Bf 109s bounce a formation of Pe-2 and Ar-2 bombers, escorted by MiG-3s, and down four of the Soviet aircraft.

28th's IAP Ivan M Kholodov, who later became a major general and a hero of the Soviet Union, believed that the Soviet fighters were too heavy to combat the Bf 109s because of their underwing machine guns. He also stated that the MiG pilots had flown too close to the bombers they were escorting,

In September 1941 Factory No 1 resumed production of MiG-3s fitted with underwing-mounted Berezin BK 12.7 mm machine guns in streamlined pods. Although these aircraft packed a heavier punch, the pods inhibited manoeuvrability and reduced the MiG-3's top speed by up to 30 km/h (18.6 mph)

From August 1941 some MiG-3s had their twin ShKAS 12.7 mm machine guns replaced with a second synchronised BS weapon of the same calibre, as the latter provided the fighter with a greater weight of fire

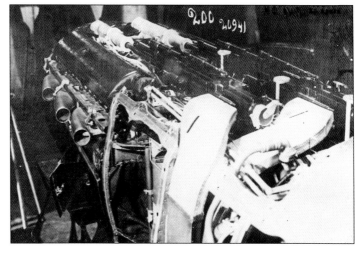

33

The inscription applied to this MiG's fuselage reads 'Death to the German invaders!' The workers at Factory No 1 wrote similar messages on many of the aircraft they built

thus making themselves an easy target for the pilots of the manoeuvrable Messerschmitts.

28th IAP would soon get its own back, however. On 8 August, Jr Lt Aleksey K Ryazanov, who would eventually receive two Hero of the Soviet Union titles, claimed to have shot a German aircraft down in flames after a protracted battle. Two days later, squadron CO Capt V B Bolovlenkov claimed to have downed two Bf 109s southwest of Kiev during the same sortie. The latter also recalled that his wingman A P Podpryatov had demonstrated equally effective performance prior to his MiG-3 going down in flames. The pilot bailed out and landed near a railway station in Solomenky, a suburb of Kiev, where he was cheered by local people. Lts A Chesnokov and V Sobolev were less lucky. The former, having received the Order of the Red Banner in early July, was killed in air combat, while the latter bailed out of his damaged MiG-3 but was strafed in his parachute.

MiG numbers in the Kiev theatre of operations steadily decreased during this period – something that could not be denied by local commanders. On 15 August, after inspecting Krasnobay airfield crammed with unserviceable aircraft, some of them MiG-3s, 44th SAD CO Col V M Zabaluev bitterly summed up the situation. 'What a cemetery!' he muttered. After that, 15th SAD military commissar Col L A Dubrovin received an order from southwestern front air force CO, Gen F A Astakhov, that by 17 August all damaged fighters, the number of which was 'growing hourly', should be repaired and made serviceable. To achieve this, a special aircraft evacuation team was formed, with repair teams appointed to every air regiment. By the 18th (officially recognised as Air Fleet Day), 38 aircraft had been restored to combat-ready status. And by the 22nd 15th SAD had 59 aircraft of various types (including seven MiG-3s, which went to 28th IAP) at its disposal.

Throughout the summer of 1941, the MiGs were also employed on diverse missions on the most southerly segment of the Soviet-German frontline. The operations included providing air support for ground troops, flying reconnaissance sorties and making tactical bombing attacks on enemy positions. But battles between the opposing forces were less frequent than in other combat zones after the invasion. Southern front intelligence summary No 23 of 6 July 1941 reported that, 'Air surveillance data indicates that enemy aircraft make only limited raids, and in small numbers, against our troops and airfields. Their strafing runs are performed by long formations in which the leading aircraft attacks with machine gun fire while those following drop bombs. The German pilots usually avoid engagements with the MiG-3'.

In general, however, the Soviet fighters' effectiveness in combat with the Luftwaffe was considered unsatisfactory by Red Army field commanders. Their complaints were summarised in an order to southern front commanders dated 25 July in which Gen I V Tyulenev pointed out that repeated raids on Soviet airfields, troop concentrations and bases in rear areas by small numbers of German aircraft had become annoying. He said he believed that the failure of Soviet fighters to intercept the attacking aircraft was caused by lack of effective ground observation. This meant that even the fastest of the available interceptors, the MiG-3s, 'are too late in taking-off, and attack enemy bombers on their way back to their own territory when they have already dropped their bombs'.

By July 1941 the southern front air force command was in a stalemate. The swift retreat of Red Army ground troops had resulted in a series of poorly arranged redeployments to remote airfields, where supplies were often unavailable or insufficient due to the limited storage capacity. Air force units were facing a shortage of fuel, spare parts and other supplies. A series of crises, including one near Kiev, resulted in the High Command being forced to redeploy a number of air divisions and regiments from the southern to the southwestern front.

For example, 146th IAP, which achieved success between 7 and 17 July, was deployed near Kotovsk and subsumed within 20th SAD. For three days the regiment was based at Khristinovaka airfield and placed under the direct control of southwestern front air force CO, Gen T T Khryukin. After that the unit was transferred to 64th SAD, with whom it remained until 14 August. The regiment was eventually redeployed from Khmelevoye to Grebenka airfields and then to Bogodukhovka.

The prolonged stay in the combat zone and the many engagements fought there helped the division's commanders accumulate combat experience and work out the most appropriate tactics for countering the Germans. These new tactics included avoiding engagements with superior

During the winter of 1941/42 personnel manning the myriad aircraft workshops immediately behind the frontline laboured around the clock to expeditiously repair and overhaul MiG fighters

An unidentified Soviet pilot strikes a customary pose for the period in front of his MiG-3

numbers of Bf 109s, being alert for sudden attacks from above, down-sun and behind, and not flying straight and level when leaving an air combat so as to avoid presenting an easy target. Pilots also received some hints about the best way of dealing with enemy bombers and reconnaissance aircraft. The main one was to knock out the gunners first.

146th IAP suffered grave losses on 11 July when a pair of fighters from II./JG 77 led by Feldwebel Rudolf Schmidt shot down squadron CO Capt O M Farafonov as he was taking-off from Voronkovo airfield. Farafonov's aircraft immediately collided with those of his two wingmen, Snr Lt Kh I Jungman and Lt V M Zaytsev. All three pilots, who were among the more experienced of the unit's aviators, having impressive combat scores, were killed and their fighters burnt out.

Soviet fighter air regiment reports indicated a decline in combat effectiveness from the second half of July onwards. Probable explanations include an abrupt decrease in the number of fighters and pilots available and the loss of the most experienced aces. Another reason was the decrease in the number of air battles. Yet there were plenty of successful engagements reported by MiG-3 pilots too. On 11 August, for example, Jr Lt V V Malov, who had already shown himself to be among the most effective fighter pilots, shot down two Messerschmitts near Kanev but was not to survive the sortie. Soon after the successful engagement, Malov suffered engine failure in his MiG-3 and was killed when the fighter nosed over as he was attempting an emergency landing in a damp meadow. Local people were frustrated in their bid to rescue the pilot when the MiG-3 exploded before they could reach it.

Two neighbouring fighter regiments, both flying MiGs on the southern sector of the Soviet-German frontline during the war's early stages, were commanded by majors called Orlov. Both 4th IAP CO Konstantin Orlov and his opposite number at 146th IAP, Vladimir Orlov, were among the highly experienced pilots who had pioneered operations with the new fighters, had led the conversion training programmes and had achieved their first victories. But while Vladimir Orlov survived the war, Konstantin was killed in a bizarre incident. At dawn on 18 August 1941, while checking the airfield guards, he was shot dead by a sentry who mistook him for an enemy spy. Orlov had five victories to his name by the time he was killed.

Many of the Soviet aces realised that they could never turn the tables on their enemy without learning the lessons of the bitter defeats they had suffered during the early stages of the war. The MiG-3s were fast and modern fighters, and they required the use of new tactics to get the best out of them. The fighting spirit that these pilots helped to generate was the fruit of their painful analysis of their own mistakes and failings, as well as a willingness to adopt some of the enemy's more successful tactics.

One such pilot to ultimately benefit from the rough handling he experienced in the MiG-3 in the early weeks of the war in the east was Snr Lt Aleksander Pokryshkin. One of his early shaves was reported in 20th SAD's operational log for 14 July. A flight of MiGs from 55th IAP was sent out to Macaresti, where it met fire from a German anti-aircraft battery. The fighter flown by Pokryshkin failed to return from the mission, a second element reporting that a MiG-3, thought to be flown by the missing pilot, had made a wheels-up forced-landing. An entry in the log three days later reported that the ace had in fact returned safely. In his memoirs Pokryshkin, now a famous fighter ace, described the desperate attempts to repair his damaged fighter, which were ultimately doomed to failure;

'In the air the MiG-3 felt light and obedient, and with a single manipulation of the controls you could easily send it wherever you wanted, adjust its position or barrel roll it. But on the ground, my aircraft, with its undercarriage retracted, was just too heavy and intractable. We fiddled around until midnight trying to lift it up so as to stand it on its wheels, but the best we could do was to rock it from wing to wing.'

Red Army soldiers arrived and helped lift the MiG-3. They tried to tow the fighter with a ZiS-5 truck, but all their efforts proved futile and the aircraft was finally burnt out. Later, during a stay in hospital, Aleksander Pokryshkin was able to think about combat tactics. He wrote;

'A retrospective review of our combat performance suggests that attacks on either ground or air targets should be made at top speed. This will make the most of the element of surprise and prevent enemy fighter and bomber pilots from making well-aimed counter-attacks, as well as protecting us from anti-aircraft fire.'

Lt Kuzma Seliverstov was one of the most effective of Pokryshkin's fellow pilots during the early days of the war. According to Pokryshkin he was 'a modest, timid and prudent individual, as well as a straight and honest comrade, a real brother in arms'. At that stage Seliverstov was probably the most successful MiG-3 pilot serving on the southern front, for he had claimed five individual victories over German (an Hs 126, a Bf 109 and a Ju 88) and Rumanian (a PZL P.24 and a P.37) aircraft, plus two more (a Bf 109 and an Hs 126) shared.

By 6 August Seliverstov had flown 132 combat sorties, prompting 55th IAP CO Maj V P Ivanov to nominate him for the title of Hero of the Soviet Union. By the end of the month the nomination had been approved by 20th SAD CO Gen A S Osipenko and 9th Army Air Force commander Gen I T Eremenko. However, by 27 March 1942, when the award was finally announced in an order of the Soviet Supreme Council, Seliverstov had long since fought his last battle. On 15 October 1941 he was killed in air combat over Sultan-Saly, 15 km (nine miles) northwest of Rostov-on-Don. Before his death he had claimed four more victories while flying the MiG-3. The day prior to Seliverstov's death another successful 55th IAP ace had also been killed in battle, Snr Lt K F Ivachev having seven individual air combat victories to his credit.

One of the best-known Soviet aces, Snr Lt A I Pokryshkin began his combat career flying the MiG-3. Serving with 55th IAP, he claimed five victories with the fighter in 1941-42

A MiG-3 from 55th IAP takes off displaying a non-standard striped camouflage scheme. Pokryshkin mentioned such colour schemes in his memoirs

THE DEFENCE OF LENINGRAD

In 1941 the city of Leningrad was one of the USSR's key industrial centres. It was also the one located nearest to what might, in the event of war, be regarded as hostile territory. Accordingly, the Soviet leadership had developed plans for the city's defence before the outbreak of war with Germany. By June 1941 the local air defences had been reorganised and re-equipped. As a result the two fighter defence air divisions, 3rd and 54th IADs, were able to field 136 I-16s and 48 I-153s, but only 30 MiG-3s.

On 23 June the Leningrad Military District Air Force command attached five more fighter air regiments to the fighter defence group based there. This meant that the four regular and five attached regiments had a total of 401 fighters (of which 339 were serviceable) and 411 pilots, including 108 qualified to fly at night. The process of converting pilots to the MiG had only just begun so that by the outbreak of war only 80 pilots were qualified on the new aircraft and just 19 could fly it at night. This in turn meant that while the handful of pilots who were on readiness at 0340 hrs on 22 June were taking off into the darkness, the remaining fighters were being hurriedly dispersed around the fields and hidden.

On 7 July the Peoples' Commissar for Defence merged all the above-mentioned units into 7th (*Istrebitelniy Aviakorpus*, IAK) of the Air Defence Force. The new CO, Hero of the Soviet Union Col Stepan Danilov, required the entire flying staff of the corps to be qualified on the MiG-3 by the 15th. A patrolling schedule was drawn up, this prescribing 24-hour two- and, in certain instances, three-tier cover of the city.

During the war's opening stages the defender's main task was the interception and destruction of German reconnaissance aircraft. The diary of 7th IAK indicates that Soviet fighters repeatedly prevented attempts by enemy reconnaissance crews to penetrate the defences of Leningrad. The I-16s and I-153s were too slow to catch the Ju 88s, which were the aircraft most frequently operated on long-range reconnaissance missions. The MiGs proved more effective at chasing them down, however, their speed enabling them to make repeated attacks on the fleeing targets.

The first kill of a German intruder in the Leningrad areas was reported on 6 July when 19th IAP's CO, Hero of the Soviet Union Maj

Future 23-kill ace Lt D S Titarenko of 19th IAP provides details of his first combat victory (a Ju 88) to Brigade Commissar F F Verov on 6 July 1941. Surviving the war, Titarenko would claim the bulk of his victories flying La-5/7s

Andrey Tkachenko, took off from Gorelovo airfield with two elements of MiG-3s to intercept yet another Ju 88 reconnaissance aircraft. One of the four Soviet pilots involved was future ace Lt Dmitry Titarenko, who managed to make two close approaches and down Ju 88D Wk-Nr. 0852. The aircraft broke up in mid-air and crashed near Bezzabotnoe. Its crew bailed out and both pilot and navigator were captured as soon as they landed. Subsequent interrogation revealed that they were members of the Luftwaffe's *Nachtaufklärungsstaffel* 2 which had been flying missions over Soviet territory long before the war had commenced.

44th IAP, which became 11th Guards IAP in March 1942, was a typical MiG-3 unit in the Leningrad area during this period. The regiment, commanded by V G Blagoveshchenskiy, noted in its diary that in July 1941 its pilots had participated in seven aerial combats and shot down two Ju 88s, four Bf 110s and six Bf 109s, all of which were claimed by aviators flying MiG-3s. The first was reported on the 8th by Lt Evstigneev. While some claims remained unsupported by corresponding German loss reports, the MiGs' combat record still appeared impressive.

By late July the frontline had moved perilously close to Leningrad. Luftwaffe bombers were particularly active in attacks on the railway station of Oktyabrskaya and the line between Leningrad and Moscow. The workload of 7th IAK's fighter pilots increased dramatically. Besides their primary objective of covering Leningrad, they were given additional assignments such as escorting trains, defending the railway line itself and flying reconnaissance and ground-attack missions. By this time many of the pilots had already developed considerable skill in air combat.

Throughout the month 154th IAP's most successful aces, Capt G V Didenko and Capt P I Pilyutov, were able to demonstrate their skill. Pilyutov was the first to claim an example of the newly-arrived German Fw 189 artillery observation aircraft, which was operated in-theatre by 1.(H)/11. Taking full advantage of his fighter's speed, another of the

A group of MiG-3s from 7th IAK fly in loose formation over central Leningrad. The high tower of the famous Peter and Paul Cathedral on the north bank of the Neva River can be seen below the fighters

regiment's pilots, Snr Lt Aleksey Storozhakov, opened his combat score on the 4th. A veteran of the 'Winter War' and the holder of two decorations, Storozhakov was nominated by 39th IAD command on 29 August to receive the title of Hero of the Soviet Union for his outstanding performance in the sky over Leningrad. By that time he had flown 152 MiG-3 combat sorties, which included 20 ground-attack, 18 reconnaissance, 37 escort and 21 interception missions. The remainder were regular patrols over the city and Oktyabrskaya station. After 25 air battles, Storozhakov had claimed six individual and three shared victories.

Some of the battles fought by these early aces were hair-raising to say the least. For example, on 6 July, while escorting a flight of SB medium bombers, deputy CO Storozhakov's two-element flight engaged a full squadron of Bf 109s and claimed to have accounted for five of them, including two attributed to the leader, for no loss. Moreover, the Germans failed to inflict any damage on the Soviet bombers. Another amazing incident involved the German attack on Torshkovichi airfield, and Storozhakov once again emerged as the hero. He had taken off while the field was under attack by four Bf 110s, engaged them, shot one down and then landed safely on the same field. And Storozhakov achieved all of this despite the loss of his rudder actuation rod. It was subsequently discovered that his fuel tank had also been punctured.

There was a particularly unusual incident on 23 July when Storozhakov was scrambled to intercept a Hs 126 reconnaissance aircraft flying over Soviet artillery batteries. The communist pilot dived out of cloud and fired at the enemy aircraft, forcing its pilot to land. Despite sustaining a minor injury, Aleksey Storozhakov landed alongside the Henschel and called on the pilot and observer to surrender. Having secured the aircraft's crew, he removed the camera and observer's machine gun from the Hs 126 and presented the trophies to his regimental CO, Col Antonov. German records confirm that Hs 126B Wk-Nr. 3355 of 8.(H)/32 failed to return from a reconnaissance mission in the area concerned, and that the crew of Oberfeldwebel A Honvelmann and Unteroffizier A Rogert were posted as missing.

A MiG-3 is refuelled under its camouflage netting at a frontline airfield near Leningrad

Of the frontline units outside the 7th IAK structure, the first regiment to switch to the MiG-3 was 159th IAP (CO Maj I A Voronin) of 5th SAD. It received 60 of the new fighters between 5 February and 25 May 1941 at Grivochki airfield. The unit's pilots had completed their conversion training by the time of the German invasion, but an investigation of the regiment's combat readiness conducted on 24/25 June by the Leningrad Military District Air Force's Aviation Engineering Service revealed a number of unwelcome facts. At Siverskaya airfield there were 23 serviceable and three unserviceable MiG-3s, while all others had either been transferred to other units or withdrawn from service for overhaul. Even those fighters that were reported as combat-ready were equipped with poorly-zeroed machine guns and substandard VISh-61P propellers, instead of the standard VISh-22E equipment. The regiment's chief engineer, Putyagin, reported that, together with an acute shortage of spare parts, shock absorber struts and heat exchangers, the regiment badly needed refuelling equipment.

From 14 July 159th IAP was subsumed within 39th IAD on the northwestern front. Early in August the regiment was reorganised into the now standard three-squadron structure. A month later one squadron was withdrawn due to equipment losses. Prior to withdrawal for replenishment on 20 September 1941, the MiG pilots had flown 2688 combat sorties and reported 34 aircraft, 12 pilots and two technicians lost. That was what it had cost to down 46 enemy aircraft and destroy 20 trucks and ten tanks. The regiment's glory was further enhanced by the heroic performance of aces such as Lts Aleksander Shevtsov and Vasiliy Schurov and Jr Lts Petr Likholetov and Vasiliy Lukin.

Most of the fighter air regiments in the Leningrad Military District had received a few MiG-3s by early July. Some, like 19th, 44th and 157th IAPs, had been scheduled for re-equipment with the LaGG-3, but those plans were abandoned in favour of the more reliable MiG-3. Other units such as 7th IAP were initially scheduled for re-equipment later in the third quarter of 1941, but they actually switched to the new fighter earlier in the summer.

7th IAP was one of the most successful units in the Finnish campaign, with seven of its pilots, including regimental CO Maj Evgeny Turenko, being awarded the title of Hero of the Soviet Union. In spring 1941 military inspector Gen A A Novikov considered the regiment's pilots to have the best flying and tactical skills in the Leningrad Military District Air Force. In accordance with regular pre-war practice, a maintenance team from 7th IAP was sent to Moscow's Factory No 1 to take delivery of the new equipment while the pilots were being trained in UTI-4 two-seaters. In early July the regiment, led by Maj Sinev, was ordered to leave Maysniemi, near Vyborg, for Gorelovo. Here, it would receive MiG-3s.

Of its most experienced pilots, 30 had been qualified on the MiG since 20 June. They were therefore able to collect the new fighters. Meanwhile, the younger pilots continued their training with I-153s at Maysniemi. And it was they who were called upon to fly the first combat sorties against the Finns in the early days of the conflict. Later, 7th IAP's pilots and aircraft were dispersed amongst a number of different units.

Pilots from 157th, 191st, 192nd and 193rd IAPs, also based at Maysniemi, found themselves under the command of Maj G M Golitsin, formerly 193rd IAP's CO, in a unit now designated 7th IAP. On 27 June nine MiG-3s of Sinev's squadron were added to the new regiment, and they departed for the first mission that day when they attacked a Finnish airfield near the village of Utti. A few days later Sinev handed the unit over to Snr Lt A A Baranov.

The first MiG victory to be confirmed by Finnish sources came on 13 July. At 0805 hrs Lt Dodonchenko of 153rd IAP intercepted and shot down a Bristol Blenheim reconnaissance aircraft at an altitude of 2000 m (6500 ft) near Lake Svirskoye. It was not until September 1942 that the Finns recovered the wreckage of the aircraft (BL-134) and the bodies of the three crew members, including the commander, Lt von Ber, near Lodeynoye Polye.

On the Karelian Isthmus the most intensive MiG activities were reported in the period from late July to the end of August 1941. 7th IAP's operations diary recorded three raids on Utti airfield on 18, 21 and 22 July, which resulted in 13 enemy aircraft destroyed either on the ground or while taking-off. These claims were not confirmed by enemy sources, however. During the first half of August, Snr Lt Baranov's fighter pilots made a series of strafing attacks on Lappenranta, Simmola, Antrea and other Finnish railway stations.

On 21 August five MiG-3s engaged an identical number of Finnish Brewster Buffalos and claimed to have shot down two for no loss. The following day two more Buffalos were claimed in an unequal contest in which three Soviet fighters were pitted against eight Finnish opponents. The Soviet pilots had overestimated their successes in their combat reports, however. For example, the nomination of Lt K D Reshetnikov for the Hero of the Soviet Union title stated that by 10 September 1941 he claimed four individual victories after 68 combat sorties, but these successes were not confirmed. Reshetnikov was killed on 19 September 1941 during an engagement with German fighters, and he was awarded the Order of the Red Banner posthumously.

Over-claiming was not restricted to the Soviet pilots. On 17 September Finnish fighter squadron Lentolaivue 24 (the only one equipped with the Brewster fighter) reported a highly successful contest with 14 MiG-3s of 179th IAP. They claimed to have shot down seven of the Russian fighters, which they reported had crashed east of the River Ladoga. For the most part that report was also the product of fighter pilots' imagination.

The archives of 179th IAP do throw some light on this particular engagement. Early in September the regiment arrived at Peski airfield north of Petrozavodsk to reinforce 7th Army Air Force. The fiercest air combat was reported to have been fought on 15 September, and to have resulted in three MiG-3 fighters being lost out of the seven engaged. Their pilots were killed. The battle began with two fighters

This MiG-3 from an unidentified regiment assigned to the defence of Leningrad in late 1941 bore the patriotic message 'For the Party of the Bolsheviks' beneath its cockpit

and their pilots, Capt Gorshunov and Political Instructor Gorbunov, being downed by Finnish fighters near Pryazha, 35 km (22 miles) northwest of Petrozavdsk. A few minutes later Jr Lt V I Strokachenko was shot down and killed by anti-aircraft fire five kilometres (three miles) west of Pryazha.

WIDENING OPERATIONS

On 12 July the MiG-3 pilots' area of operations spread further north with their redeployment to 147th IAP in Karelia. Having received the order to deliver ten MiG-3s from a Leningrad suburb to an airfield 1000 km (625 miles) further north, the head of the Leningrad Military District Air Force Aviation Engineering Service, Brigade Engineer A V Ageyev, was authorised to fly the aircraft to their destination rather than send them by train so as to avoid unnecessary delays.

The pilots had to fly over hundreds of kilometres of uninhabited forest devoid of notable landmarks. Another difficulty was that the formation included earlier MiG-3 variants with 640-litre (140 gal) fuel tanks, as well as later examples with 450-litre (99 gal) tanks. For acceptance purposes, a special team of seven technicians, seven engine specialists and an equipment specialist was assembled at Murmashi airfield, near Murmansk, to inspect the new arrivals. After that, 7th IAP pilots ferried the entire fleet safely to their ultimate destination via Kolezhma, near Belomorsk, and Afrikanda, near Kandalaksha, where they refuelled. They were led by Lt P S Kutakhov, who would soon become an ace and after the war go on to be Air Force Commander-In-Chief.

Archive reports indicate that by mid July 147th IAP had just four MiG-3s, and that they were operated by Capt F A Gruzdev and selected pilots who had been given the task of intercepting enemy bombers. By the end of the month a further 17 new MiG-3s and six specially trained pilots had arrived. Fighting alongside the best aviators from 147th IAP, such as L P T Zelenov (one individual and two shared victories by the end of 1941), they gave a good account of themselves in the Afrikanda and Loukhi regions.

Of the units that defended Leningrad from its furthest outposts, 15th IAP was among the most distinguished. Having lost its entire complement of aircraft in the initial German onslaught, the regiment arrived at Dyagilevo, in the Ryazan Region, on 4 August to receive new fighters. 15th IAP had well-trained pilots, half of whom already had ten to forty flying hours on MiG-3s to their credit. By the 14th the pilots had completed their conversion training, with each of them having at least ten hours of flying time to their names. The evaluation commission appraised as excellent the flying skills of the regimental commander, who had logged a total of 800 hours, and deputy squadron commander, Snr Lt A A Dmitriev, who had 775 flying hours. Capts M V Kuznetsov and V A Churinov and Snr Lt A E Vasin also received high marks for their performance. It was not surprising, therefore, that these pilots would soon be among the most prominent Soviet aces.

Conversion training reports, however, suggested that a pilot's pre-war experience was no guide to his ability to master the new aircraft. For example, the skills of one squadron commander, Capt V Y Evtyukhin, were rated only as 'satisfactory', despite his 1520 flying hours. On the other hand, relatively inexperienced Lts I N Pashko, N A Musienko and G I Nikanorov received 'good' marks for their skills with the MiG, even though they only had about 150 flying hours each to their credit. In general, 15th IAP was judged ready for combat.

The regiment was subsumed within 8th SAD and deployed on the northwestern front. Soviet documents reported that in late August there was a series of raids on enemy airfields south of Leningrad, including those at Lisino, Zarudinye and Spasskaya Polist. The striking forces usually comprised LaGG-3 and MiG-3 fighters, some of which carried rocket projectiles and bombs, while the others provided escorts for the improvised attackers. On 25 August six MiGs of 15th IAP visited Lisino after the airfield had already been bombed by 46th IAP, whose pilots reported the destruction of four Messerschmitts.

That evening the German airfield at Spasskaya Polist was hit hard. Having considered all the pilots' reports, 8th SAD concluded that 35 to 40 German aircraft had been destroyed on the ground. Another 14 had been hit during their take-off runs and a further six shot down once they had become airborne. In addition, four fuel storage tanks were set on fire. Soviet losses amounted to eight fighters. On the other hand, no confirmation of these losses could be found in German reports, leading to the conclusion that the strike had probably resulted in six to eight aircraft of II.(Schl)/LG 2 being destroyed on the ground. An AO-25 fragmentation bomb exploded close to Bf 109E Wk-Nr. 3455 and set it on fire, while another weapon accounted for Bf 109E Wk-Nr. 0926. Some airfield facilities were also reportedly damaged.

Earlier that same day a handful of MiG-3 pilots claimed victories after an aerial battle near Spasskaya Polist, Snr Lt A A Dmitriyev intercepting and shooting down a Bf 110 of *Stabstaffel* StG 1, which was based here. Both crewmen bailed out and landed safely after delaying the opening of their parachutes. A month earlier Dmitriyev had been the subject of a Soviet Information Bureau report stating that 'the invincible fighter ace' had 'shot down 11 fascist aircraft during the first month of the Great Patriotic War'.

In an analysis of the MiG-3's combat deployment south of Leningrad, 8th SAD CO Col N S Toropchin stressed that despite

Pilots from 15th IAP conduct a debriefing for the benefit of the camera following a combat sortie over the northwestern front in September 1941

Pilots and groundcrew from an 8th SAD regiment come together for a group photograph on the northwestern front in late 1941

the basic variant's lack of firepower from its two small-calibre and single large-calibre machine guns, the MiG-3 had proved to be the 'strongest and most durable' of all the new fighter types. Armed with supplementary rocket projectiles, the aircraft could, Toropchin believed, become a most effective weapon against enemy bombers and ground troops. 'The MiG-3 aircraft has demonstrated good flight and combat performance', the divisional commander continued, but he added, 'The clear disadvantage is the fighter's poor manoeuvrability at low altitudes. The MiG's manoeuvrability below 2500-3000 m (8125-9750 ft) makes it inferior to the Me 109, and it is too slow to fight the Me 110'.

Skilled pilots could, of course, take advantage of the fighter's strengths. By exploiting its excellent vertical performance they could bounce an enemy aircraft from above. Taking into account the fact that ranking MiG-3 ace Snr Lt A A Dmitriyev had fought the latest Bf 110E-3 (Wk-Nr. 2403), his low-level victory on 25 August was a remarkable achievement. The outcome of the engagement was mainly determined by the Soviet pilot's ability to force the German crew into a disadvantageous position soon after take-off. The Messerschmitt had become an easy target for the Soviet ace.

THE HARDEST DAYS

Late August and early September were the hardest days for the defenders of Leningrad, as the enemy had commenced its decisive assault. The Luftwaffe redeployed VIII *Fliegerkorps* to *Luftflotte* 1, and by doing so secured domination in the air. It was also able to provide strong support to German ground forces. From 8 September onwards, the only routes of communication with the besieged city were by air or across Lake Ladoga. The Wehrmacht advanced on the suburbs of Kolpino and Krasnogvardeysk and attempted to cross to the right bank of the Neva so as to join up with Finnish troops on the Karelian Isthmus. This would complete the city's envelopment.

A MiG-3 squadron commander (with map) from an 8th SAD regiment briefs his pilots in the field south of Leningrad

To counter this desperate situation, all air arms, including MiG-3-equipped units, were subordinated to the joint command. Now they were dedicated to providing air cover for the defending ground troops. With patrols over the city halted, flights of MiG-3s were now frequently tasked with attacking German troops encircling the city. The Soviet fighter pilots suffered many losses during this period. On 10 September, for example, Snr Lt A N Storozhakov, holder of the Order of Lenin and two Orders of the Red Banner, was killed in combat. He was made a posthumous Hero of the Soviet Union.

By mid October an alarming situation was developing east of Leningrad. German troops were advancing on Tikhvin to complete a second envelopment of the city. The Soviet Command ordered the local air forces to weaken the enemy as much as possible through air strikes, and to this end the Leningrad Front Air Task Force was formed on 16 October with 79 combat-ready aircraft. This

Pilots from a 7th IAK regiment walk away from a snowy dispersal on the the Leningrad front during the winter of 1941/42

A well-weathered MiG-3 of 519th IAP prepares for take-off

number doubled with the arrival at Tikhvin of Col E Y Kholzakov's 3rd Reserve Aviation Group (*Reservnaya Aviatsionnaya Gruppa*, RAG) with dozens more MiG-3 fighters.

It was not an easy task to weld them all into a single group because most of the reserves were drawn from the Moscow area. All the constituent units urgently required replenishment too, especially those with the newer aircraft. Leningrad Front Air Force chief engineer, Brigade Engineer A V Ageyev, watched the CO, Gen A A Novikov, personally decide the destination of each arriving fighter. On 7 October Novikov distributed the remaining aircraft of the withdrawn 158th IAP among the other units (7th IAK and 123rd, 127th and 563rd IAPs) still in the frontline.

When the offensive on Leningrad was eventually countered the enemy withdrew a significant number of aircraft to other theatres. Yet despite the decrease in intensity of flying operations, the Soviets reported a major increase in aircraft losses. This might have been due to a change in activity by the German fighter forces. No longer were they supporting ground troops and escorting bombers targeting the supply route over Lake Ladoga. Instead, they were hunting Soviet transport aircraft and their escorts. Many experienced pilots were to die during those days, including Snr Lt Dmitriyev of 15th IAP in an air battle on 13 November.

At the time of Dmitriyev's demise, 15th IAP was based at Levashova as part of the Leningrad Air Defence Force. Having just downed a Messerschmitt near Nevskaya Dubrovka, east of the city, Dmitriyev's section was bounced by a second Bf 109 flown by ace Hauptmann Heinrich Jung of I./JG 54, who killed or disabled the Soviet ace with a single well-aimed burst of fire. The MiG-3 crashed, its pilot having made no attempt to escape. So died the most successful MiG-3 pilot.

In less than five months of combat Dmitriyev's score had risen to 15 individual and two shared victories (as well as an observation balloon). At the time of his death, he was the holder of the Order of Lenin and the Order of the Red Banner, having received the latter award after completing more than 800 operational flying hours.

Seven more pilots from Dmitriyev's regiment were reported killed or missing in November.

Of the entire complement of MiGs that had been deployed to defend Leningrad back in August, only one aircraft (serial number 4097) remained serviceable by the end of the month. According to 8th SAD headquarters, the losses highlighted the risk of flying so many missions at minimal altitudes in poor weather, these factors combining to drastically reduce the MiG-3's manoeuvrability. Furthermore, the worn-out state of so many aircraft restricted their pilots' ability to exploit the fighters' strengths.

This brand new MiG-3, displaying a winter camouflage scheme, features the inscription 'For the Party of the Bolsheviks'. It was just one of three patriotically marked MiGs photographed during a ceremony at Moscow's Factory No 1 on 23 February 1942 – Red Army and Navy Day

All that and more was applicable to 41st IAP, which was brought in to reinforce the Volkhov Front Air Force in early 1942. No other fighter regiment could match the ability of Lt Col V S Yershov's pilots, who had had ample time to become familiar with the MiG. The regiment, having re-equipped with MiG-1s and then MiG-3s in January 1941, fought on the western front between 22 June and 5 July and then was transferred to Moscow Air Defence until 13 August. 41st IAP had then been posted to the northwestern front, where it served until 5 October.

It was at a critical point during the defence of Moscow that 41st IAP was formally attached to the Western Front Air Force. One of its squadrons, however, was placed under the personal command of Moscow Military District Air Force CO, Col N A Sbytov. A further squadron remained in the VVS RKKA Military Council's reserve pending the start of the counter offensive in the Moscow area. Soon after the Red Army began its counter offensive on all the fronts 41st IAP was redeployed to the Leningrad area. The High Command initially subordinated the regiment to the commander of the Volkhov Front 59th Army Air Force, but in early February it became part of Col E G Turenko's 2nd RAG to support the 2nd Attack Army's offensive on Myasnoy Bor and, later, Lyuban.

Pilots of 41st IAP read *Pravda* in what is obviously a posed photograph taken by a frontline journalist during the defence of Moscow in August 1941

It might appear from official Western Front Air Force documentation that the Soviet command had concentrated enough force with 26 air regiments and several independent units to win control of the air. However, most of the regiments were under-equipped and their aircraft outdated.

Before the redeployment, 41st IAP reported that its pilots had flown 3332 combat sorties totalling 2875 flying hours, most of them with MiGs, between 22 June 1941 and 28 January 1942. Their most frequent tasks included supporting

troops, strafing the enemy and intercepting Luftwaffe raids. These missions totalled 1070, 870 and 598 combat sorties, respectively. The regiment claimed 83 German fighters shot down, plus a further 24 destroyed on the ground. 41st IAP's most successful MiG pilots as of 28 January 1942 were;

Rank and Name	Sorties flown	Individual victories	Shared victories
Snr Lt I D Chulkov	187	11	1
Snr Lt A A Lipilin	128	5	3
Snr Lt D G Korovchenko	168	7	-
Snr Lt P A Tikhomirov	119	7	-
Snr Lt P I Zabelin	151	2	3
Col V S Ershov	70	2	1

On the basis of these results, the regimental commander nominated the most successful pilots, Chulkov and Lipilin, to receive the title of Heroes of the Soviet Union. Also nominated were Capt S A Skornyakov and Snr Lt I G Kuzmichev, who had flown, respectively, 62 and 57 raids targeting enemy troops, vehicles and airfields. They had also jointly accounted for seven enemy aircraft destroyed on the ground. By the time this nomination was made, however, Kuzmichev had been posted missing in action.

A shortage of serviceable MiGs, even after the completion of all necessary repairs, forced 41st IAP to operate a mixed fleet of 17 MiG-3s (the latest variant with two BS machine guns) and six Yak-1s from early February 1942. To make matters worse, these few precious fighters were widely distributed across six airfields. The regiment's technical personnel had reported that airframes and powerplants were worn out, with the AM-35A engines of the 2nd squadron's fighters having no more than 28 per cent of their lives left. So most of the equipment required major overhaul even before the unit had started flying from its new location.

Tragedy had befallen 41st IAP prior to its arrival at the Volkhov Front, Jr Lt Frimerman's engine failing en route to the Leningrad area. He was killed in the ensuing crash. The unit's initial operations from Gremyachevo airfield were also dogged by accidents, most of which were due to the poorly prepared runway. Between 2 and 6 February, five of the 44 combat sorties flown ended with MiG-3s plunging into the snow upon landing and being damaged.

41st IAP's heaviest loss came on 3 February when Snr Lt I D Chulkov, the regiment's most successful pilot, failed to return from his 201st mission. He was last seen in his badly damaged MiG-3 descending towards Malaya Vishera. It is possible that Chulkov was finished off by fellow ace

MiG-3s lacked heated cockpits, so operations in cold weather required pilots to wear a suitable flying suit and fur-lined boots

A damaged MiG-3 undergoes repair at a frontline workshop of the Leningrad Front Air Task Force

Oberleutnant Heinz Lange of I./JG 54. German reports for that day indicate that a free-hunting element sighted a lone Soviet fighter emitting smoke. They quickly shot it down, the leader of the German pair claiming the aircraft as his 11th kill. Confirmation of Chulkov's death arrived on 18 February, and on 4 March the unit was notified that he had been awarded the title of Hero of the Soviet Union. Lipilin received his award at the same time.

Yet there were more losses due to accidents than to enemy action during this period. Indeed, statistics reveal that only on 5 February were that day's two reported losses both due to combat. Snr Lt Kuzmichev was injured when he crash-landed his battle-damaged MiG-3 in the forest after he had managed to reach Soviet-held territory. Lt Popov was able to bail out of his burning fighter. All other losses were due to equipment failures or defects. On 18 February the regimental engineer reported that the lives of all the unit's AM-35A engines were now exhausted.

In late February and early March the Germans began an intensive regrouping of their ground forces along the hard-surface roads. Their intention was to launch attacks on the flanks of the Soviet 2nd Strike Army advancing on Lyuban. Communist attempts to prevent this with a series of attacks from the air proved ineffective. This failure was partially explained by the units' poor state of combat readiness.

A review of accidents occurring during training flights and combat sorties on the Volkhov front between 1 January and 15 March by the air force chief engineer revealed 542 failures with equipment malfunctions. There had been 256 instances of defective workmanship on airframes and engines, and pilots and groundcrew were held responsible for 132 accidents. The remaining cases were attributed to design defects. The report also included some unwelcome statistics about reliability. The MiG-3, together with the Pe-2 bomber, had suffered the majority of the failures at the Volkhov front. After 74 days of operations, the relatively small number of MiG-3s involved in combat were responsible for 232 reported accidents and instances of malfunction. This implied a failure rate of more than three a day. The grievances of crews about this state of affairs were understandable. Operations by all aircraft types were affected by poor weather, but it was noticeable that while Yak-1s, U-2s or R-5s were able to fly, the MiG-3s would be grounded awaiting repair.

It was clear what action was required. All frontline fighter units were re-equipped with Yak-1s, while the remaining MiGs were withdrawn to the rear. The days of the MiG-3 as a frontline fighter were over.

MiG-3 fighters run their engines up prior to take-off in 1942, the nearest machine bearing the inscription 'Death to the German Invaders!'

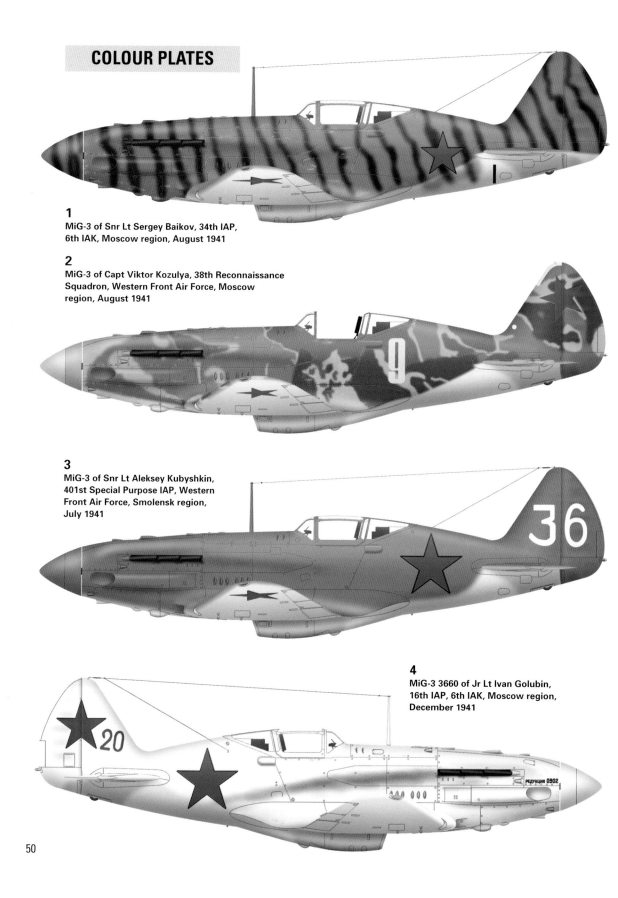

1
MiG-3 of Snr Lt Sergey Baikov, 34th IAP,
6th IAK, Moscow region, August 1941

2
MiG-3 of Capt Viktor Kozulya, 38th Reconnaissance
Squadron, Western Front Air Force, Moscow
region, August 1941

3
MiG-3 of Snr Lt Aleksey Kubyshkin,
401st Special Purpose IAP, Western
Front Air Force, Smolensk region,
July 1941

4
MiG-3 3660 of Jr Lt Ivan Golubin,
16th IAP, 6th IAK, Moscow region,
December 1941

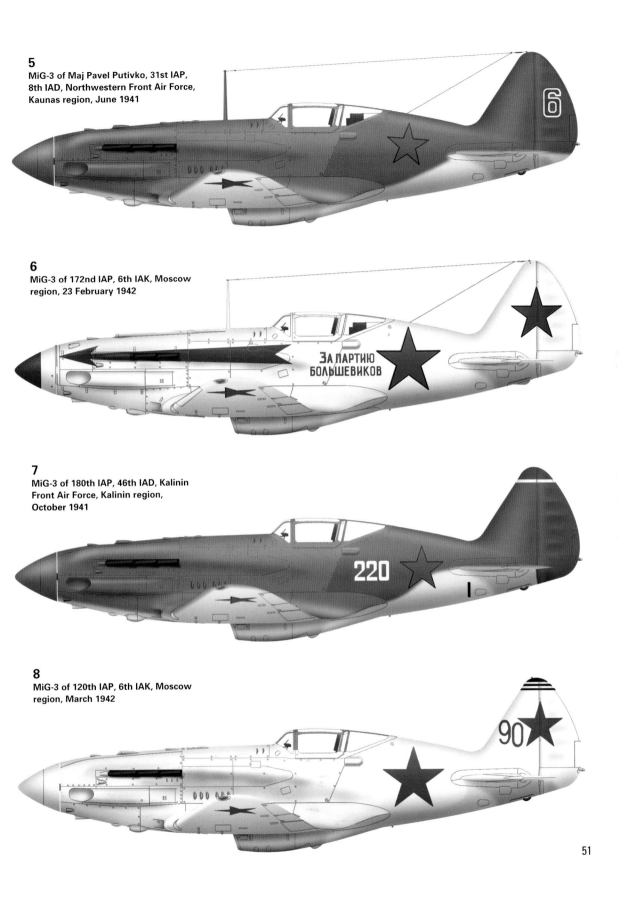

5
MiG-3 of Maj Pavel Putivko, 31st IAP,
8th IAD, Northwestern Front Air Force,
Kaunas region, June 1941

6
MiG-3 of 172nd IAP, 6th IAK, Moscow
region, 23 February 1942

ЗА ПАРТИЮ
БОЛЬШЕВИКОВ

7
MiG-3 of 180th IAP, 46th IAD, Kalinin
Front Air Force, Kalinin region,
October 1941

8
MiG-3 of 120th IAP, 6th IAK, Moscow
region, March 1942

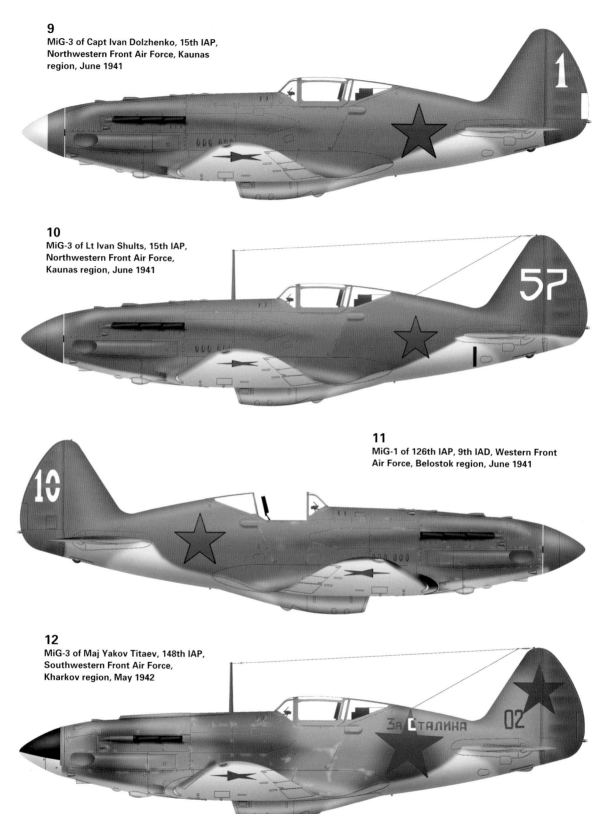

9
MiG-3 of Capt Ivan Dolzhenko, 15th IAP,
Northwestern Front Air Force, Kaunas
region, June 1941

10
MiG-3 of Lt Ivan Shults, 15th IAP,
Northwestern Front Air Force,
Kaunas region, June 1941

11
MiG-1 of 126th IAP, 9th IAD, Western Front
Air Force, Belostok region, June 1941

12
MiG-3 of Maj Yakov Titaev, 148th IAP,
Southwestern Front Air Force,
Kharkov region, May 1942

13
MiG-3 of Capt Ivan Rybin, 148th IAP,
Southwestern Front Air Force,
Kharkov region, June 1942

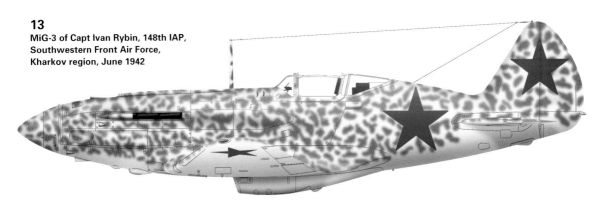

14
MiG-3 of Snr Lt Aleksander Lipilin,
41st IAP, 6th IAK, Moscow region,
August 1941

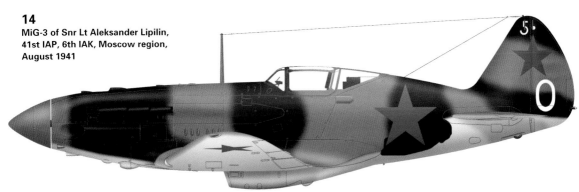

15
MiG-3 of Snr Lt Mikhail Nekrasov,
148th IAP, Southwestern Air Force,
Kiev region, September 1941

16
MiG-3 of Lt Aleksey Nikitin, 7th IAP,
Leningrad Front Air Force, Leningrad
region, October 1941

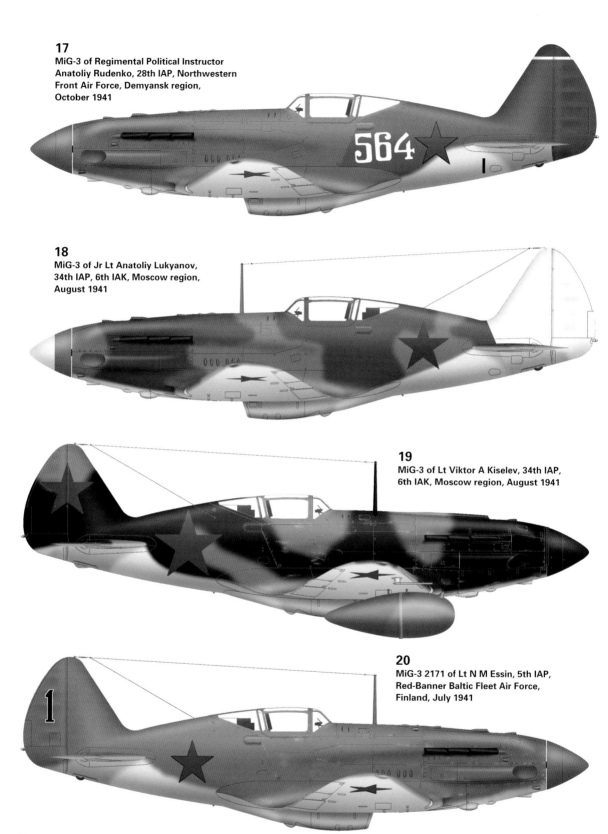

17
MiG-3 of Regimental Political Instructor
Anatoliy Rudenko, 28th IAP, Northwestern
Front Air Force, Demyansk region,
October 1941

18
MiG-3 of Jr Lt Anatoliy Lukyanov,
34th IAP, 6th IAK, Moscow region,
August 1941

19
MiG-3 of Lt Viktor A Kiselev, 34th IAP,
6th IAK, Moscow region, August 1941

20
MiG-3 2171 of Lt N M Essin, 5th IAP,
Red-Banner Baltic Fleet Air Force,
Finland, July 1941

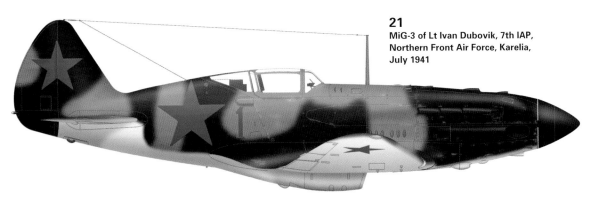

21
MiG-3 of Lt Ivan Dubovik, 7th IAP,
Northern Front Air Force, Karelia,
July 1941

22
MiG-3 of Snr Lt Aleksander Shevarev,
31st IAP, Northwestern Front Air
Force, Kaunas region, June 1941

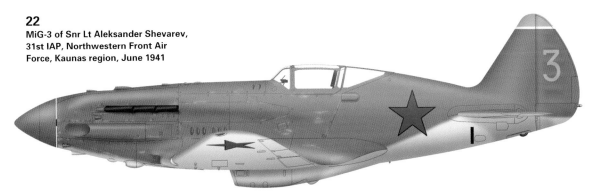

23
MiG-3 of Capt K D Denisov, 7th IAP,
Black Sea Fleet Air Force, Tuapse
region, August 1942

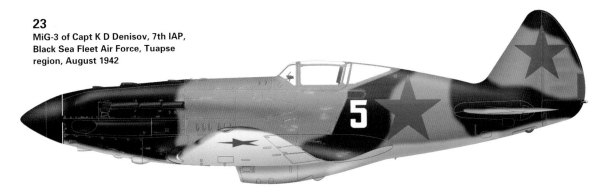

24
MiG-3 of Capt S N Polyakov, 7th IAP,
Leningrad Front Air Force, Leningrad
region, September 1941

25
MiG-3 of Capt Aleksander A Sharmin,
7th IAP, Black Sea Fleet Air Force,
Kuban region, May 1943

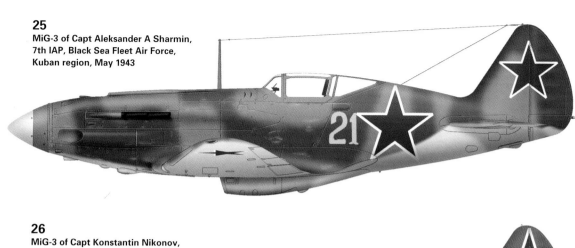

26
MiG-3 of Capt Konstantin Nikonov,
7th IAP, Black Sea Fleet Air Force,
Caucasus region, July 1943

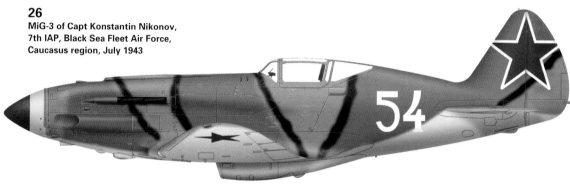

27
MiG-3 of Snr Lt Kuzma Seliverstov,
55th IAP, Southern Front Air Force,
Beltsy region, June 1941

28
MiG-3 of Jr Lt Grigoriy Gorban,
185th IAP, 6th IAK, Moscow region,
March 1942

29
MiG-3 of Jr Lt Grigoriy German,
42nd IAP, Western Front Air Force,
Moscow region, August 1941

30
MiG-3 of Lt Mikhail Baranov, 183rd IAP,
Western Front Air Force, Moscow
region, December 1941

31
MiG-3 Capt Ivan Zabolotny, 16th IAP,
6th IAK, Moscow region,
February 1942

32
MiG-3 of Lt Ivan Kholodov, 28th IAP,
6th IAK, Moscow region,
February 1942

HEROES OF MOSCOW

Right from the start of the war MiG-3s and other Soviet fighters were flown on regular patrols by 6th IAK of the Air Defence Force. This was a special organisation whose sole purpose was the air defence of Moscow. However, by the end of June 1941 the only interceptions being made were of friendly aircraft that had inadvertently flown into the Moscow Air Defence Zone. Such flights were strictly prohibited, and the interceptions were due to poor coordination and communication between the errant aircraft and ground controllers. On a more serious note, these incidents exposed a lack of effective measures to counter enemy intrusion into the city's airspace. Indeed, experienced Luftwaffe crews found it easy to conduct photo-reconnaissance missions over Moscow at altitudes of 8000-10,000 m (26,000-32,500 ft).

Thanks to its rate-of-climb and good high-altitude performance, the MiG-3 was considered to be the fighter best suited to the task of intercepting the intruders. But lack of information from ground observers frustrated attempts to prevent the incursions, which continued even when the weather was completely clear. However, the air defence organisation was improving, and the first MiG victories over German reconnaissance aircraft were attributed by the Moscow Zone Air Defence Staff to 126th IAP, commanded by Lt Col Yuri Nemtsevich, which operated at the outer limits of the region.

The regiment had entered the war as part of 9th SAD, but that formation was soon dispersed and the regiment redeployed to Gomel. There, it was placed under the command of Western Front Air Force deputy commander-in-chief Gen A I Tayursky. When he was sacked, the regiment was transferred to 21st Army Air Force, commanded by Gen G A Vorozheykin. From there the unit was quickly redeployed to the Moscow Air Defence Force. Soviet archives indicate that after two months of continuous combat, the regiment's pilots were credited with destroying 147 enemy aircraft both in the air and on the ground. As a result, 29 pilots were decorated.

MiG-3 pilot Lt V G Kamenshchikov and I-16 pilot Jr Lt S G Ridny were made Heroes of the Soviet Union on 9 August. One of Vladimir Kamenshchikov's victories was over a Bf 109, which had been escorting bombers sent to

MiG-3s fly a low-level patrol over Moscow's Red Square in the summer of 1941. This is either a staged shot, taken from the roof of the Moskva Hotel, or a photographic sketch

attack a railway junction on the western perimeter of the Air Defence Zone on 7 July. This is thought to have been the first victory attributed to a 6th IAK MiG-3.

Meanwhile, the citizens and defenders of Moscow were anxiously waiting for the inevitable night bombing onslaught. This duly commenced on 21 July, when 195 bombers from 12 different Luftwaffe groups set out for Moscow as ordered by the *Führer*. He had instructed the bomber crews to raze the city to the ground. Waiting for them were 173 patrolling Soviet fighters, of which 40 were MiGs. This was an impressive number given that prior to the completion of a recent, intensive, three-week training programme, only eight pilots in the whole corps had been qualified to operate the MiG-3 at night.

The following day the Supreme Commander-in-Chief praised all those who had been involved in defending the Soviet capital. In Order No 0241 of 24 July, the Peoples' Commissar for Defence, Joseph Stalin, summed up the way the first raid had been rebuffed. Two days after that it was announced that 17 military pilots were to be decorated. Among recipients of the Order of the Red Banner were four MiG-3 pilots, Snr Lt P V Eremeev (27th IAP), Jr Lts A G Lukyanov and N G Scherbina (both 34th IAP) and M K Baykalov, a civilian test pilot working for the Flight Testing Institute of the Peoples' Commissariat of the Aviation Industry. All four had fought in air battles and claimed to have shot down enemy aircraft during the first month of the war.

There were further attacks in the period up to 11 August 1941. During that time all participants in the city's air defences – particularly fighter pilots – did their best to thwart the raiders. The German command soon acknowledged the futility of mounting such massive attacks, and restricted the raids to smaller formations of bombers. Most of the attacking aircraft were required for tactical purposes in the frontline, such as supporting the advancing land forces.

During this period many Soviet fighter pilots claimed notable nocturnal victories, although most were overly optimistic when it came to measuring their success. One example came in a report to the commander of 6th IAK by 34th IAP CO, Maj L G Rybkin. Summarising the outcome of aerial engagements fought between 21 and 27 July 1941, the report included the statement;

'On his second night sortie on 22 July, at about 0240 hrs, between Alabino and Naro-Fominsk, at an altitude of 2500 m (8125 ft), Capt M G Trunov pursued a Ju 88 and attacked it from behind. The enemy descended to a low level and Capt Trunov lost sight of his opponent, having left him far behind and below. The enemy aircraft may therefore be considered as shot down.'

Subsequent reports from Rybkin and other commanders contain phrases like 'direct hits could be

34th IAP CO Lt Col Rybkin and his deputy for political activities, Battalion Commissar Nedrigaylov

Only the most experienced pilots were able to fly night missions in the MiG-3, which lacked flame suppressors on its exhaust stubs

These MiG-3s are flying in the standard early-war formation, with the leader in front and his two wingmen to the side and slightly behind. If a sudden turn was required the inner wingman found himself in an awkward position, being forced to slow down, which meant lagging behind the rest of the formation once it had levelled out again

seen from the ground', 'the enemy may be judged as shot down' and 'no confirmation of the victory from ground observers has yet been received from the frontline'.

The ability of German aircraft to survive damage was impressive, the He 111 in particular often demonstrating its ability to withstand dozens of hits and keep on going for long distances on one engine. This survivability was helped by the Soviet pilots' lack of knowledge of the weak points of the opposing aircraft and the location of their defensive machine guns. This meant that they usually preferred to attack from longer ranges rather than closing in before firing. Decisive attacks with the relatively light weapons then used by Soviet fighters were not that easy, especially as bomber crews were continually refining their tactics.

The Soviet aviation staff were continually preoccupied with improving their tactics too, as well as rationalising the organisation of the city's defences. Moscow Military District Air Force commander Col N A Sybtov reported to the district commanding general, P A Artyomyev, that 1st Air Defence Corps, which essentially comprised the anti-aircraft artillery batteries deployed in and around Moscow, repeatedly procrastinated in halting its barrage and then giving clearance for fighters to enter the airspace over the city centre. This delayed the defending fighters' interception of the raiders in an operational environment that required continuous patrolling by 12-18 MiG-3s within a 5000-7000 m (16,250-22,750 ft) envelope. Sybtov wrote;

'At higher altitudes, fighters experience predictable difficulties in attacking non-illuminated targets, but in any case the probability of a pilot finding and shooting down a bomber is much higher than that of an anti-aircraft battery achieving the same outcome.'

Many still argued that anti-aircraft artillery was sufficient to cover the city centre, and there were claims that deploying fighters hastily prepared for nocturnal operations would be too risky. In his report, Lt Col P M Stefanovsky, deputy CO of 6th IAK, wrote that, 'The MiG-3 is poorly equipped for night operations, and this has already resulted in major losses'. Among the main risks, according to Stefanovsky, were pilots being

dazzled by flames from engine exhausts, a lack of radio direction finders and gyro horizons, insufficient fuel capacity and other design deficiencies.

Furthermore, thorough scrutiny of nocturnal combat missions undertaken by staff officers revealed systematic errors and faults by pilots in the control of aerial engagements, the sighting of enemy aircraft and the preparation and conduct of their initial attacks. The report's somewhat trivial conclusions included a recommendation to avoid shooting at night from long range, together with the need for better communication between airborne and land-based defences. It therefore had to be admitted that the few confirmed instances of a successful deployment of fighters at night were attributable to courage and luck, rather than to any systematic approach to countering night raids on Moscow. One such engagement was detailed in a report to 6th IAK CO Col I D Klimov by 124th IAP's commander, Maj A Pronin;

'At 1710 hrs on 7 August 1941, having received a report from the command post at Tula airfield of an unidentified aircraft heading for Moscow via Sukhinichi at high altitude, my deputy, Capt Kruglov, took off in a MiG-3 to investigate. At 1730 hrs, having climbed up to an altitude of 7000 m (22,750 ft)

Pilots of 124th IAP, which was involved on the defence of Moscow during the second half of 1941. These men are, from left to right, Dmitriy Zanin, Aleksander Pronin, Nikolay Tsisarenko and Grigoriy Ivanchenko

More pilots from 124th IAP pose in front of a well-concealed MiG-3

124th IAP squadron commander Capt Aleksander Pronin pictured in a reflective mood sitting on the wing of his MiG-3

Snr Lts Nikolay Tsisarenko (left) and Mikhail Barsov stand in front of a weathered MiG-3. Tsisarenko would become one of 124th IAP's highest-scoring fighter pilots

and commenced patrolling near Myaskovo, he saw a condensation trail at about 8000 m (26,000 ft) and immediately received a message that the target was above him. Having climbed to that altitude, Kruglov failed to detect the target. A few minutes later the pilot sighted an approaching dot above and ahead of him. The dot was swiftly approaching, and having identified it as an enemy aircraft, he opened fire from a range of 300-500 m (325-540 yards) in a head-on attack. Raising the nose of his aircraft to avoid a collision caused the port wing of the MiG-3 to stall as the enemy bomber passed within 100-150 m (110-160 yards). The German crew had probably not seen Capt Kruglov because there was no defensive fire.

'Capt Kruglov levelled his fighter, climbed again and made another attack, approaching from behind and to the right of the bomber. After two further lengthy bursts, the enemy aircraft's right engine began smoking. The lower gunner returned fire and Kruglov took violent evasive action, before hitting the bomber with two more bursts from a range of 200-300 m (215-325 yards). At this point the enemy aircraft tried to hide in a cloud, and the Soviet pilot attempted to finish it off from close range by hitting the other engine. Despite the damage, the bomber disappeared into thick cloud and Capt Kruglov failed to follow. He then descended to 2000 m (6500 ft), but could not find the enemy aircraft and returned to his base near Tula.

'Post-flight visual inspection of the MiG-3 found one puncture hole in the fuselage. All of its 7.62 mm ammunition had been expended, as had 70 per cent of the 12.7 mm ammunition prior to failure of the synchronising mechanism of the right-hand ShKAS gun, which will require replacement.'

Nicolay Kruglov's attack had been successful. This was confirmed by the local internal affairs authorities, who reported that the German aircraft had made a forced-landing near Maloyaroslavets, whereupon its crew was captured. Kruglov was nominated for the Order of the Red Banner. The citation noted that he had also claimed to have shot down a Do 215 near the national border on the first day of the war in the east. According to German documents, two Bf 110s (another twin-engined aircraft with twin fins and rudders) had been lost near Zambrow on 22 June, while Do 215B Wk-Nr. 0068 of the Luftwaffe's *Aufklärungsgruppe* 1 had been shot down on 7 August. The Dornier's intended route had been Bryansk-Kaluga-Roslavl-Bryansk. However, the crew deviated to the east and their aircraft was intercepted. The entire four-man crew, led by the navigator, Leutnant J Babick, was captured.

During the summer of 1941 the names of the MiG-3 pilots who had achieved success in the night sky over Moscow were widely reported in the Soviet press. These men also acted as role models for those who had just completed their training on the fighter. Among them were Snr Lt V A Kiselev of 34th IAP, who brought down an He 111 in a ramming attack on 10 August, and Lt A N Katrich of 27th IAP, who downed a Do 215 the following day. The latter used his propeller on the Dornier while flying at 8000 m (26,000 ft), but was still able to get his fighter home without it suffering any further serious damage. This was the first reported high-altitude ramming attack of the war.

The engagement had started when Aleksey Katrich took off from an airfield near Kalinin and sighted a vapour trail while he was climbing. He followed the trail, still climbing, and soon sighted the target aircraft. Katrich caught up with it over Bologoye railway junction when his altimeter was showing 7500 m (24,375 ft). Over preceding days other pilots of 27th IAP had chased a reconnaissance aircraft, but they had failed to catch it. There was some speculation that Katrich's victim, which he reported as a Do 217, had been the earlier intruder. Now, having reached Bologoye, the enemy aircraft abruptly turned southeast and followed the straight Leningrad-Moscow railway line.

The Soviet pilot finally fell behind the enemy and came within firing range at 8000 m (26,000 ft). From 100 m (110 yards) he fired a long burst with all his guns, stitching the Dornier's fuselage from tail to wing. The left engine started smoking. There was no return fire and the enemy aircraft went into a dive. Katrich attempted another burst but his guns misfired, probably due to overheating. Continuing the pursuit, he decided to make a ramming attack rather than let the enemy aircraft go.

Before the war Katrich had been a regular participant in annual military parades, where he demonstrated precise formation flying skills. Relying on these techniques, but now in a combat situation, he flew an approach that allowed him to close in on the Dornier and then hit it. Seconds later he throttled back and turned steeply to port to avoid hitting the stricken German aircraft. Its pilot tried to level out, and he seemed to have succeeded by the time the bomber was at 600 m (1950 ft). However, a minute later the aircraft tipped into an uncontrolled dive and crashed near Staritsa, killing the four-man crew. The photographic equipment was extracted from the wreckage and taken to Moscow.

Katrich not only landed safely but was able to taxi his fighter back to its dispersal area, even though two propeller blades were found to have been bent inwards. When he inspected the wreckage of his victim, he asked if he could take the aircraft commander's pistol and jacket (with its display of medal ribbons) as souvenirs.

In September the frequency of aerial engagements and reports of victories in the Moscow area declined. This could to some extent be explained by the cessation of the massive Luftwaffe air raids. Air Defence Force reports state that only ten German aircraft were destroyed in September, and the actual number lost was probably less than that. Three of the claims were made by MiG pilots who had rammed enemy reconnaissance aircraft. One of them was Jr Lt N L Grunin of 124th IAP. He reported

Snr Lt V A Kiselev of 34th IAP helped repulse the German air raid on Moscow on 10 August, bringing down an He 111 in a ramming attack

These young sergeant pilots from an unidentified MiG-3 regiment in 6th IAK were photographed between missions during the early days of the war

ramming Ju 88A Wk-Nr. 0587 of 4.(F)/11 using the wing of his MiG-3. He was forced to bail out of his burning fighter as a result.

Five days later one of Grunin's fellow pilots reported a less dramatic episode. Having attacked Ju 88D Wk-Nr. 1271 of 1.(F)/33 west of Tula at 7000 m (22,900 ft), Jr Lt B G Pirozhkov failed to bring it down – he had fired all his ammunition and damaged the Ju 88's tail with his propeller. Pirozhkov was able to coax his damaged MiG-3 back to base. Meanwhile, the crippled enemy aircraft dived to 1800 m (5850 ft), levelled off and continued flying. Pirozhkov's wingman, Jr Lt V I Dovgiy, decided to make another ramming attack. This time the Ju 88's tail was seriously damaged and the aircraft crashed. Dovgiy force-landed near the village of Khanino.

On 28 September 171st IAP pilot Jr Lt G N Startsev rammed a solitary He 111 over Skuratovo railway junction in the Tula region just as the enemy aircraft made a bombing run on a troop train. A perfectly delivered attack resulted in only slight damage to the MiG-3, however, Startsev being able to make it safely back to his base. The Heinkel probably also survived because no corresponding loss reports could be found in the Luftwaffe Quartermaster-General's log.

FORMATION OF 177TH IAP

By the end of September 1941 ten regiments of 6th IAK were able to report a strength of 175 MiG-3s out of a total 459 available. A single fighter was also attached to its headquarters. Just before the decisive events in the protracted battle for Moscow, the Soviet Command established a few more MiG-equipped regiments, to which it posted some of the most experienced pilots. One 27th IAP squadron was restructured and transferred to 177th IAP, with its CO, Maj M I Korolev, being promoted to command the regiment

177th IAP had been formally established on 18 May 1941. A month later its few surviving I-16s were transferred to 11th, 34th and 120th IAPs. Soon afterwards 42 sergeant pilots – recent graduates of expedited wartime flying training courses – joined the regiment. Its commanders now had to get these novice pilots into a combat-ready state as soon as possible. Training commenced at Dubrovitsy airfield, near Podolsk, using UTI-4s and I-16 fighters, with the most promising trainees being rostered for night patrols.

On 31 August 177th IAP entered a new era when Battalion Commissar N L Khodyrev made the unit's first MiG-3 night flight. In doing so he also made it clear that such practical demonstrations by party officials were often the best form of persuasion when it came to training junior pilots. Khodyrev and Korolev followed up by managing the instruction of their less experienced colleagues. Usually, it took four to six weeks to develop all the necessary flying and combat skills for the MiG-3. 'Although some pilots, such as Lts Rubanov and Feklyunin and Sgts Evstratov and Vorobyev, required more flying practice, and despite some equipment breakdowns, all trainee pilots would eventually become true aces', 177th IAP's official history noted somewhat optimistically.

With MiG-3s having replaced half of the regiment's complement of obsolete aircraft, nine pilots were considered ready for combat operations by the end of September. Following the start of the German offensive,

34th IAP pilot S I Platov claimed a handful of successes in the MiG-3, and later became one of the regiments most successful aviators

Korolev's unit was attached to 77th SAD to begin operations in the southern defensive sector. The regiment's MiG-3s began flying regular patrols of the Moscow-to-Warsaw road, and on 13 October the first claim was made when Snr Lt Samodurov and his wingman Jr Lt Muravyev reported shooting down an Hs 126. As this engagement proved, the expedited pilot training programme had resulted in 177th IAP being ready for the German autumn offensive on Moscow.

The Western Front air arm included 180th and 129th IAPs, while the Bryansk Front air arm had 274th and 42nd IAPs. The latter regiment, having lost its entire strength in the early days of the war during operations from its base near the Baltic coast, had been re-formed by late July under the command of Hero of the Soviet Union Fedor Shinkarenko. He had been given *carte blanche* to recruit the best graduates of the elite flying school at Kacha, near Sevastopol, and they were appointed squadron and flight commanders. He also took the cream of 126th and 129th IAPs and 6th Reserve IAP.

On 16 August High Command HQ ordered 42nd IAP and its three squadrons to start patrolling in the Bryansk and Orel areas with their MiG-3s. That order was issued immediately after the unit had completed an intensive training course during which its 32 pilots had made 1422 flights and logged 287 flying hours on MiG-3s. The regiment was able to report that, 'On 18 August 1941 squadron commander Snr Lt Vlasov exhausted all his ammunition during an engagement with a Ju 88 and was forced to resort to a ramming attack. The German aircraft was destroyed and its crew were killed. Snr Lt Vlasov was wounded while making a forced-landing'.

In July 1943, now a lieutenant colonel and a Hero of the Soviet Union, N I Vlasov was taken prisoner after landing on an airfield near Leningrad that had just been captured by the Germans. He eventually died in January 1945 during his second attempt at escaping from Mauthausen concentration camp in Austria.

Of his engagement on 18 August 1941, German sources reported that a Do 215 reconnaissance aircraft of *Luftflotte* 2 had been seriously damaged in the impact with Vlasov's fighter near Verkhopolye, southeast of Bryansk, but had managed to land safely at its base. Most of the other victories claimed by 42nd IAP pilots were not acknowledged by the Germans, indicating perhaps that mastering the MiG-3 and using it effectively in combat had not been an easy task for the regiment's novice aviators. This would appear to be confirmed by the pilots' choice of I-16s and I-153s for night operations – some of these older fighters were repaired examples abandoned at Orel by previous occupants.

On 30 September Bryansk Front aviation units had a strength of 62 fighters, exactly half of which were MiG-3s. When the enemy began a sudden offensive followed by a swift advance from the south towards Moscow, the Soviets were forced to withdraw to avoid the risk of their aircraft falling into enemy hands. Even the prompt redeployment of 6th RAG to the threatened area proved only a partial remedy.

Following its spell on the Bryansk Front in August, this group, commanded by Gen A A Demidov, and with MiG-3-equipped 42nd IAP as its most effective unit, had been held in reserve and tasked by supreme command headquarters with a variety of *ad hoc* missions. Compared with

Jr Lt Viktor Talalikhin of 177th IAP is believed to have been the first Soviet pilot to make a ramming attack on a German aircraft at night when, on 7 August 1941 while flying an I-16, he brought down an He 111 over Moscow. Made a Hero of the Soviet Union for this feat and feted by the press, Talalikhin subsequently flew the MiG-3 until he was killed in combat over Podolsk on 27 October while leading a mixed group of two MiG-3s and six I-16s. Having been seen to shoot down two Bf 109s, Talalikhin fell victim to a third German fighter. A veteran of the Winter War with Finland, during which he claimed three victories during the course of 47 sorties, he had claimed a further five kills by the time of his death neighbouring 425th and 509th IAPs, 42nd IAP's pilots had greater proficiency with the MiG-3s when thrown back into action.

In the uncertain frontline environment of early October 1941, reconnaissance missions were considered to be the MiG-3 pilots' top priority. The German *Typhoon* offensive had had a negative impact on the Soviets, whose top commanders lacked data to make reliable estimates of either the enemy's forces or plans. And commanders of the western, Bryansk and reserve fronts were unable to meet this pressing need.

Available reports suggest several probable sources for the crucial information provided to the Red Army on the breakthrough at Vyazma by German motorised troops. The first to spot the continuous flow of Wehrmacht tanks and trucks on their way to Yukhnov at dawn on 5 October were probably Pe-2 crewmembers Majs G P Karpenko and D M Gorshkov of the Moscow Military District air force. The Western Front's intelligence summary, however, attributed the first report to 10th IAP MiG-3 pilot Lt Zavgorodny. His post-flight report timed at 1415 hrs states that, 'A convoy of 30 to 40 tanks and 30 to 40 trucks with soldiers, accompanied by a few fuel tankers and armoured vehicles, passed across our airfields at Klimovo and Znamenka to the rear of the western front. The convoy was escorted by 18 to 20 fighters'.

Contemporary reports suggest that, having detected enemy troops on the move, many MiG-3 pilots proceeded to deliver effective ground strikes, slowing the pace of the offensive.

In poor weather, the fighter's performance in the ground attack role often depended as much on the availability of proper navigation equipment as it did on the skill of the pilot. The corps command repeatedly asked the higher military authorities for prompt shipments of radio direction finders to enable at least some fighters to fly at night or in bad weather. On 9 October, 6th IAK staff commander Col I I Komarov asked VVS RKKA chief navigator Gen B V Sterligov to send 65 RPK-10 radio direction finders for his MiG-3s, but there is no indication that this request was met. 27th IAP did, however, receive such equipment in sufficient numbers to fit them to all the squadron commanders' MiG-3s. This regiment was one of the longest-established of the Moscow air defence units, 36 of its 53 pilots having converted onto the MiG-3 by the outbreak of war. Nevertheless, even they lacked sufficient combat experience with the new aircraft, and none had attempted to fly it at night.

The diversity of missions flown during the summer and early autumn of 1941 – reconnaissance flights, transport escort, intercepting intruders, patrols of railway junctions and some special missions – enabled most pilots to quickly gain thorough experience of the new fighter.

In the second half of October 27th IAP's pilots began an intensive series of air combat and ground attack sorties. By that time the regiment's MiG-3s had been modified to launch rocket projectiles. Pilots were called upon to fly several sorties a day and cover an air defence sector from Volokolamsk in the northwest to Mozhaysk, Medyn, Maloyaroslavets, Kolomna and, further south, Kashira.

During this period 16th IAP was also heavily involved in the defence of Moscow, and three of its lieutenants all called Ivan – I N Zabolotny, I F Golubin and I P Shumilov – emerged as some of the most successful

MiG-3 aces. All would be awarded the title of Hero of the Soviet Union after the German defeat at Moscow. The award was made under an order dated 4 March 1942, but it would be posthumous in Zabolotny's case. Claiming his first victory on 12 October when he downed a Ju 88 near Voskresensk, Zabolotny had flown 110 combat sorties and reportedly scored ten individual victories by the time of his death on 4 January 1942.

When the war started Golubin was serving as a staff officer because of injuries sustained during a recent forced-landing. He was eager to return to active service and, even before his transfer to another unit, Lt Golubin had flown 134 combat sorties and claimed nine individual and two shared victories. He was also among the first to pioneer the use of rocket projectiles.

Ivan Shumilov flew MiG-3s with 16th IAP for the first 18 months of the war, completing an astounding 565 combat sorties and claiming seven individual and two shared kills. On 2 December 1941 he achieved the unique distinction of downing two Ju 88s with a single rocket launched from his under wing rack. He survived the war with a tally of 16 and two shared victories to his name.

It is not possible to give a complete description of the individual air battles over Moscow because there were too many fought in the autumn of 1941. Whenever the weather permitted, dozens of fierce engagements were reported every day along the defence line, many involving MiG-3 pilots. In most reports the achievements of the VVS RKKA were overstated, so what follows represents a small number of actions in which the Soviet victory claims were confirmed by German documents.

34th IAP's official historical records note that 22 October 1941 was a special day, stating that 'pilots flew 59 combat sorties and reported 24 aerial engagements in which 12 enemy aircraft were shot down. No bombers were allowed through'. The regimental diary states that seven victories were confirmed but two MiG-3s were lost. One crash landed, while the other pilot reported a successful ramming attack on an enemy aircraft, resulting in the destruction of both. He bailed out but no wreckage of the German bomber was ever found.

The *Luftflotte* 2 reported flying 624 sorties that day, and acknowledged the loss of 20 aircraft, including 13 Ju 88s and He 111s. It is probable that Maj L G Rybkin's pilots decimated the KG 53 bomber formation, which reported losing seven He 111s to Soviet fighters

Slogans applied to the fuselages of Soviet fighters were chosen by the regiment's political staff or by the citizens or members of the collective who had donated the funds to pay for the aircraft. In this case, the message reads 'For Stalin'. Note the white winter camouflage and the red arrow displayed on the side of the fighter

T G Belousov of 34th IAP was another MiG-3 pilot who resorted to ramming a German bomber over the Moscow area in order to bring it down

Hero of the Soviet Union and high-scoring ace Capt K A Kryukov of 12th Guards IAP (formerly 120th IAP) poses with his fighter

16th IAP ace S V Achkasov, who fought on the Voronezh front, used his MiG-3 to down two German bombers (one by ramming) in October 1941

between Odintsovo and Nemchinovka. Surprisingly, most of the Soviet pilots identified their victims as Ju 88s, possibly because of poor visibility in adverse weather. One of the participating Soviet pilots was Lt Z A Durnaykin, who recalled;

'Immediately after take-off I had to climb through a thick blanket of cloud, but soon found myself above it. I then sighted, briefly, the shape of the Ju 88 not far away. "You're dead, viper", I thought, and followed him until he disappeared again into the clouds. A few minutes later he popped up from the thick mist. He was just where I was expecting him to appear – some 80 m (90 yards) in front of my fighter. So I just pushed the gun button and fired three long bursts into him. The enemy aeroplane burst into flames and crashed near Aprelevka railway station.'

On 27 October Capt A M Vinokurov of 171st IAP claimed two Bf 109s and a Bf 110 destroyed during a single engagement. The Germans acknowledged two of the losses. That same day 120th IAP, which had no more than seven or eight serviceable aircraft, reported flying 21 ground attack sorties out of a total of 56 flown near Serpukhov and Volokolamsk by regiments equipped with MiG-3s and Il-2s. Many pilots, including Snr Lt V M Tomilin, Lt I I Bocharov and Lt N N Stuchkin, all of whom had recently converted from the I-153 *Chaika*, each flew five combat sorties and claimed to have inflicted damage on the enemy forces.

Some MiG-3 sorties ended in painful defeat, however. On 29 October 423rd IAP was redeploying from Myaskovo to Volyntsevo – both near Tula. A superior force of Bf 110s surprised the unit's pilots immediately after they had taken-off and forced them into an uneven battle that resulted in the deaths of Jr Lts V Dovgy, A Denisenko and N Zabolotny. Although Soviet reports indicated that all three had brought down an enemy fighter before they too were shot down, German sources confirmed the loss of only one aircraft from II./SKG 210.

On that day 6th IAK MiG-3 units were involved in many intensive aerial engagements, as well as performing ground attack missions in several different areas. Finally, pilots also had to intercept one of the last major bombing raids on Moscow. The corps reported 16 fighters and three aviators lost, with eight more posted missing, including MiG-3 pilot Jr Lt Kryuchkov of 171st IAP. He would soon be rescued though, having managed to put his badly damaged fighter down safely in German-held territory. Disguised as a local peasant, Kryuchkov escaped, only to then spend ten days under arrest until Internal Affairs officers were satisfied by his answers and returned him to his regiment.

In early November 6th IAK summarised its units' performance during the defence of Moscow to mark the forthcoming 24th anniversary of the Great October Socialist Revolution. The four most successful MiG-3-equipped air regiments were reported to be 34th, 27th, 16th and 233rd IAPs, whose achievements were as follows;

Regiment	Enemy aircraft destroyed	Aircraft lost	Pilots lost in the air	Pilots lost on the ground	Pilots lost in combat	Other pilot losses	Total Repairable
34th IAP	51	?	18	15	33	17	9
27th IAP	36	25	13	4	17	10	9
16th IAP	43	?	5	4	9	7	3
233rd IAP	31	?	23	5	28	9	13

The above data is not limited to MiG-3 successes and losses. For example, the combined strength of 27th and 233rd IAPs indicates that many reported victories could be attributed to I-16 pilots. Nevertheless, the regiments that pioneered MiG-3 combat operations in the VVS RKKA are all represented in this list.

During the second half of October 28th IAP entered the theatre. On the 13th its new MiG-3s, each equipped with two large-calibre machine guns, arrived at Monino airfield. The unit became part of 6th IAK and immediately went into action, but unlike those regiments in the air defence forces that suffered many unnecessary losses due to inexperience with the MiG-3, its pilots were able to demonstrate their better combat skills and tactical training. During the summer of 1941 they had gained much combat experience while fighting against different German aircraft types on the southwestern front. By the end of October, therefore, the regimental CO, Maj N F Demidov, could report that 28th IAP had claimed six aerial victories and eight enemy aircraft destroyed on ground for the loss of just one MiG-3 whose pilot was able to bail out safely.

6th IAK's hardest day was 14 November when it reported flying 51 combat sorties. During a single prolonged engagement with Bf 109s from I./JG 52, seven MiG-3s were lost and five pilots posted missing. Six of the fighters were brand new machines, representing the latest variants built by Factory No 1. Two aircraft made forced landings and two of the missing pilots were subsequently admitted to field hospitals.

Among 28th IAP participants were several future aces, including Evgeny Gorbatyuk, Ivan Kholodov and Aleksander Fedorov. While the Soviets claimed eight victories,

MiG-3 pilot Snr Lt A E Fedorov of 28th IAP was awarded the title of Hero of the Soviet Union in 1942 following his participation in the defence of Moscow the previous year. He claimed his first two victories in the MiG-3

This view of Snr Lt A E Fedorov shows him wearing typical apparel for a Soviet fighter pilot in the winter of 1941/42

This MiG-3 of 172nd IAP displays the message 'For the Motherland'

German documents acknowledge only the loss of two Bf 109Fs (Wk-Nrs. 8188 and 8985). One German pilot was taken prisoner. The documents state that during a hard-fought air battle the German commander, Oberleutnant Helmut Bennemann, managed to use his radio to organise his Messerschmitt elements at different altitudes in order to make the best use of cloud cover so as to deliver surprise attacks.

The details reported by the commander of 171st IAP for an action dated 26 November were somewhat sketchy. Soon after noon the unit was preparing to leave Ryazhsk airfield for redeployment to Kashira. At this point a Bf 110 passed over the field and dropped some small delayed-action bombs, which eventually caused casualties among ground personnel. A short while later a message arrived from 6th IAK deputy commander P M Stefanovsky ordering fighters aloft to intercept an approaching enemy reconnaissance aircraft. Regimental commander Lt Col S I Orlyakhin himself responded by taking off in a MiG-3 to chase the intruder. The other pilots then left for their new airfield, where all landed safely bar Orlyakhin, who was reported missing.

Over the next few days 171st IAP was out of communication with higher command. Once a radio link was restored, the unit was notified that Orlyakhin had landed at Kashira on 2 December, the delay being explained by a forced landing due to engine failure at another field. No details of his encounter were available, but the Germans reported that Oberstleutnant Friedrich Pasquay and his crew were posted as missing from a reconnaissance mission to Tambov on 26 November.

On 19 and 20 December, during the successful Soviet counter-offensive near Moscow, 6th IAK once again reported its latest achievements, this time to celebrate Stalin's birthday. Of the corps' total fleet of 558 aircraft, the MiG-3 remained the most numerous type – six regiments had a total of 143 serviceable and 66 unserviceable examples. There was even a solitary MiG-1 on 27th IAP's strength. Compared with the prescribed establishment, there was a shortage of 106 fighters.

In the period between 22 June and 20 December 1941, 6th IAK's active inventory was replenished by the arrival of 361 MiG-1/3s. Of these, 41 aircraft were eventually transferred to other operational units and 111 were written off. Combat losses amounted to 74 MiGs, including

62 in air combat, six shot down by anti-aircraft fire, five destroyed in ramming attacks and one that crashed when its pilot lost control after being dazzled by a German searchlight. Non-combat losses included 15 due to malfunctions that were attributable to pilot error. Only one of the latter ended fatally, the pilot failing to recover his MiG from a dive. All the other casualties were associated with crash landings.

While particular attention has been paid in this chapter to the combat performance of 6th IAK, regular frontline pilots were also involved in the defence of Moscow in addition to those of the Air Defence Force. Regular VVS RKKA fighter units often shared airfields with their air defence counterparts and performed essentially similar tasks, especially in the period between October and December 1941. Most frontline and army fighter air regiments had already suffered severe equipment losses by the autumn, and could at best field just one combat-ready MiG-3 squadron each. The prevailing situation would not allow any reinforcements.

Groundcrewmen push a heavily stained MiG-3 from 6th IAK back into its camouflaged shelter on the Moscow front in late 1941

THE MOST EFFECTIVE ATTACK

Among the few MiG-equipped VVS RKKA units, 42nd and 180th IAPs both made tangible contributions to the struggle for control of the skies over Moscow. The achievements of 42nd IAP have already been discussed in some detail, but the events of 11 October should be singled out. The regiment reported that 12 Il-2 ground attack aircraft and six MiG-3 escorts destroyed 60 enemy aircraft at Orel West airfield and shot down nine more while the Germans were trying to counter the raid. The authors have been unable to find any other example of missions in which there was such effective participation by MiG-3 units.

A group of fighter pilots led by Capt G V Zimin was briefed to escort the Il-2s and, if possible, assist in the destruction of enemy machines on the ground. In his report, Zimin stated that he sighted more than 200 German bombers parked wingtip-to-wingtip on the airfield. He immediately signalled the other attackers to follow his dive onto the target. The Il-2s, led by 74th Ground-Attack Aviation Regiment (*Shturmovoy Aviapolk*, ShAP) commander Capt S E Sentemov, followed the fighters. The Soviet aircraft duly made three to four firing passes each. In addition to the destruction on the ground, the Soviet pilots claimed to have shot down four Bf 109s as they took off and five Ju 52/3m transports that were making landing approaches.

German reports stated that while the losses suffered by III./JG 3 were insignificant, II./StG 77's dive-bombers were hard hit. More serious was the impact on KGrzbV 9, which lost two Ju 52/3ms (Wk-Nrs 6870 and 6988) which had been carrying much-needed supplies to an advanced airfield. The crews bailed out and survived, but a third Ju 52/3m (Wk-Nr. 6356) crashed near the airfield, killing its crew. The total losses to Oberst Martin Fiebig's unit, which was operating south and southwest of Moscow, could be estimated as at least ten to twelve aircraft.

A witness to these attacks was Hauptmann Egon Stoll-Berberich of StG 77, who stressed the determination of the Soviet pilots conducting the attack on Orel West airfield. He believed that if the attackers had chosen to approach from down-sun, they could have achieved complete surprise and inflicted even more damage. With their extended formation manoeuvre, the Soviet fighters and ground-attack aircraft revealed their presence, thus giving the enemy air defences enough time to prepare. Stoll-Berberich stated that the pilots' tactics reflected their intention of escaping back to Soviet-held territory immediately after the raid.

It is, however, possible that Stoll-Berberich had been confused and was actually describing another Soviet raid made during the afternoon of 11 October. 42nd IAP's commander, Capt F I Shinkarenko, recalled that 'some of the 6th RAG commanders must have felt elated by the success of the first raid as they ordered another on the same day in defiance of common sense'. The enemy, of course, was fully alert and able to shoot down four MiG-3s and four Il-2s. Most of the downed pilots bailed out and eventually reached friendly territory.

Summarising the key elements of 180th IAP's performance, it may be concluded that its pilots played an important role in the defence of Moscow. On 8 August 1941 the regiment arrived at the western front to begin operations as part of 46th SAD. It comprised three squadrons, two of which were completely equipped with MiG-3s. By October pilots and groundcrew were short of supplies, and they were forced to move base four times within a fortnight as German troops rapidly advanced towards Moscow. Finally, on 13 October, unit CO Capt A P Sergeev was shot down by groundfire while landing – the enemy had just captured 180th IAP's airfield. Sergeev was succeeded by Capt I M Khlusovich.

Future regimental aces like Capt V V Novikov-Ilyin, Snr Lt I S Pasechnik and battalion commissar V I Zinoviev demonstrated the highest combat effectiveness. They would soon become widely known and serve as role models for pilots far beyond the western front. It was not, therefore, surprising that in November 1941, with the enemy close to Moscow's outskirts, the ten most successful pilots were recommended for decorations. They included Maj S I Timofeev and Hero of the Soviet Union A F Semenov, who both received the Order of Lenin and the Order of the Red Banner within a month.

A notable episode was reported on 30 November 1941. After a short engagement involving seven MiG-3s and nine Bf 109Fs near Solnechnogorsk, which cost each side one aircraft, then ranking 180th IAP ace Jr Lt S V Makarov managed to make an emergency landing on an

These MiG-3s were still in service with 565th IAP in 1943

abandoned airfield near Klin, which was then in enemy hands. His wingman and friend, Jr Lt S F Dolgushin (also a high-scoring MiG-3 ace), noticed that German motorised troops were heading towards the field so he landed nearby. Makarov promptly climbed into Dolgushin's cockpit and the improvised 'two-seater' took off under enemy fire.

Sergey Makarov would go on to fly 260 combat sorties and claim ten individual and 13 shared victories prior to his death in combat on 10 February 1942. Sergey Dolgushin flew about 180 combat sorties and claimed eight individual and two shared victories in the MiG-3 – he would survive the war with 17 and 11 shared victories to his credit. On 10 February 1942 both pilots (Makarov posthumously) would be nominated to receive the title of Hero of the Soviet Union. The award, made by the Supreme Council of the USSR, was dated 5 May 1942.

There are many examples of the courage and selflessness displayed by Soviet fighter pilots during the autumn of 1941 in the defence of Moscow. Their perseverance in the face of hardships, multiplied by the courageous efforts of thousands of infantrymen, tank crews and artillery personnel, helped to frustrate the Germans in their efforts to capture the Soviet capital. And it was at the gates of Moscow that the Red Army inflicted the first major defeat on the Wehrmacht, in the process dispelling the myth of Nazi invincibility.

Flying some of the last MiG-3s still in service, these pilots of 34th IAP conduct a quick briefing prior to heading out on a combat sortie on the Moscow front in the spring of 1943. This regiment subsequently replaced its weary MiG-3s with brand new Yak-9s

By the end of November the Luftwaffe had lost complete control in the air. The role of the MiG-3 as the symbol of Soviet success in the air during the autumn and early winter of 1941 could not be exaggerated. Despite suffering heavy losses at the hands of the enemy, the fighter had performed extraordinary feats in the skies over Moscow.

NAVAL MiGS

The very nature of the conflict between the Soviet Union and Germany made it an essentially land war. This meant that naval fighter pilots were often required to carry out similar missions to their regular frontline VVS RKKA counterparts, such as supporting troops and escorting bombers and attack aircraft, as well as performing their normal role of protecting ships and naval installations and escorting convoys.

There were four naval fleets subordinated to the Peoples' Commissar of the Navy, and each had its own air arm equipped with hundreds of aircraft. The Black Sea and Baltic fleets operated the greatest numbers of MiG-1/3 fighters.

Black Sea Fleet documents indicate that just before the start of combat operations in the theatre, Soviet battleships and aircraft had just completed a series of major combined manoeuvres. The complicated international situation forced the Peoples' Commissar of the Navy, Adm N G Kuznetsov, to place his crews and ships on alert – his order was issued at 0055 hrs on 22 June. At the main fleet base of Sevastopol this meant recalling all personnel from leave or otherwise off duty. Aircraft and crews were rapidly brought to a state of readiness.

Just after 0400 hrs that same morning, pilots of 32nd IAP, based at Kacha and commanded by Maj N Z Pavlov, took off to patrol the nearby coastal area. However, by that time five (some reports say nine) He 111s of II./KG 4, which had earlier departed the Rumanian airfields of Focsani and Buzau, had dropped mines in the channel leading to the mouth of Sevastopol Bay, effectively blocking it to shipping. When the Soviet fighters arrived the German aircraft were already heading for home. Nobody could now be in any doubt that the war had started.

32nd IAP had received its first MiGs when, just a few days before the outbreak of war, 16 fighters had been accepted from Factory No 1 by naval flying officers. Although one MiG-1 and two MiG-3s had been assembled and flight-tested at the local airfield, the remaining airframes were still in their crates by 22 June. The new fighters were intended for the squadron commanded by Capt Ivan Lyubimov, but none of its pilots were qualified to fly the MiG. As a result, both Lyubimov and his wingman, Mikhail Avdeev (soon to become a well-known ace) took off for their first wartime patrol flying old I-16s.

On 27 June Adm Kuznetsov made a bleak assessment of these initial combat operations, concluding that pilot training on the MiG-3 had been inadequate. Training would therefore soon intensify to enable 32nd IAP to take full advantage of all 16 of its new generation fighters.

During the first days of the war naval fighter pilots were kept busy covering the key fleet installations on the northwestern shore of the Black Sea, as well as defending Odessa. Enemy aircraft rarely approached Sevastopol during daylight hours, which meant that the fighter pilots' key duty at this time was to prevent nocturnal reconnaissance incursions and repeated attempts to mine the bay.

The outcome of first air battles showed that even pilots who had completed extensive pre-war training programmes were unable to coordinate their activities with other units, especially when they were based at different airfields. It was also clear that more practice in night operations and working with anti-aircraft searchlight batteries was required. Only the more experienced aviators were allowed to fly combat missions with the MiGs until the end of July.

The first volume of *The Chronicles of the Great Patriotic War of the Soviet Union in the Black Sea Theatre* contains a report dated 23 July 1941 which states that, 'In an aerial engagement above the main Black Sea Fleet base an Me 109 was shot down – our own losses amounted to one MiG-3'. This entry begs the question of how a Bf 109 would have had the range to reach Sevastopol. Three days later, the same source described an incident involving a flight of MiGs taking off to intercept enemy reconnaissance aircraft. The outcome was not reported, however, and there is no indication as to whether any losses were incurred.

Other sources contain a somewhat vague reference indicating that the first ramming attack in the Black Sea theatre occurred on either 23 or 27 June when a MiG-3 or a LaGG-3 encountered either a Dornier or a Heinkel. According to the Central Naval Archive, the first ramming in the theatre occurred on 23 July when the MiG-3 of Lt Evgraph Ryzhov, accompanied by his wingman, Lt P Telegin, pursued an enemy reconnaissance aircraft that attempted to escape by flying out to sea. Having exhausted his ammunition, Ryzhov used his propeller to chop the tail of the intruder and was then forced to ditch into the sea. It was three days before Ryzhov was rescued by a boat from a Soviet convoy heading for Odessa. The Luftwaffe Quartermaster-General reported that Do 215, Wk-Nr. 0011 of the *Aufklärungsgruppe* was missing from a mission to Sevastopol on that date. The four-man crew, led by Oberleutnant Julius Shulze-Plozius, was probably drowned.

Naval MiG fighters made a tangible contribution to the defence of the Crimea against German attacks. By early September, 29 MiG-3s were operated by 9th and 62nd IAPs, which were part of the Black Sea Fleet Special Air Group (*Osobaya Aviagruppa*, OAG). Formed on 14 September, this unit operated from six airfields southwest of Dzhankoy. Called the Fraydorf Air Group after its main base, on the day it was established the Black Sea Fleet Air Force reported that six MiG-3s operating within a 14-aircraft formation took part in a bombing and strafing raid in support of a counterattack by the 9th Army.

A MiG-3 fighter of 8th IAP, Black Sea Fleet Air Force, in 1941

The Fraydorf Air Group operated several different aircraft types ranging from the newest Il-2s and Yak-1s to obsolete I-5s. In the last week of September naval fighter pilots flew 2127 sorties, including about 200 with MiG-1/3s, and dropped some 389 tons of bombs on enemy positions. Soviet crews reported shooting down 70 enemy

This MiG-3's engine is about to be started the hard way – using an elastic rubber cord. Two men, one of them the squadron CO, are holding the engine's crankshaft, allowing the cord to stretch

This 9th IAP MiG-3 hit trees while making a forced-landing following engine failure shortly after take-off

aircraft, destroying 19 tanks and 231 motor vehicles and silencing six anti-aircraft batteries. In addition, they claimed to have accounted for 24 enemy aircraft on the ground. The cost of this effort was 37 aircraft lost, including five MiG-3s.

During this period the MiGs often took off with bombs, which they dropped on enemy troop positions at the bottlenecks of Chongar and Perekop, even though the commander of the Black Sea Air Force believed that I-16s were better suited to the role of improvised ground attack aircraft. The Soviet pilots' high level of activity worried the Germans, and Gen Erich von Manstein, who commanded the Wehrmacht offensive, reported that the Soviets had gained temporary air superiority. In mid October the Luftwaffe transferred Bf 109F-equipped III./JG 52 and II./JG 3 to an airfield north of Perekop, where they joined three other similarly-equipped units. The entire German tactical air wing was put under command of Oberst Werner Mölders, Inspector General of Fighter Air Forces.

The Soviet command decided on a reorganisation to improve the management of its forces. This included transferring the Fraydorf Air Group to the 51st Detached Army Air Force, commanded by Col V A Sudets. Yet by early October Soviet forces found themselves in a badly deteriorating situation. Reconnaissance missions were flown by MiG-3s, but unlike the I-16s, they lacked cameras. This meant that pilots were restricted to making visual reports of what they had observed. Particular attention was paid to the roads in the isthmus of Perekop, along which armoured and motorised infantry units advanced into Soviet territory. These sorties were flown by single aircraft, and the risks were high. Indeed, in the first three weeks of October no fewer than eight MiG-3s failed to return from reconnaissance missions.

Another was lost after making a ramming attack on 18 October, Lt N I Savva of 32nd IAP downing a Do 215 of the *Aufklärungsgruppe* near Balaklava. Savva had copied Ryzhikov's exploit of 23 July, and he too had to be rescued after ditching in the sea. Savva was later awarded the Order of the Red Banner.

Evgraph Ryzhikov, also of 32nd IAP, was the most successful MiG fighter pilot in the Black Sea theatre. Regimental records state that on 31 October he shot down a Ju 87 and a Bf 109 near the Sevastopol suburb of Kacha. By November Ryzhikov's victory tally had risen to five, and he would go on to claim 11 individual and five shared victories, most of them while flying the MiG-3. A serious wound received during an air battle grounded him in October 1943.

Despite November's thick fog and heavy rain, the Soviet airmen remained operationally active. Few sorties were flown by the MiG-3s, however, due to a chronic shortage of serviceable fighters. Although there were few aircraft available to patrol the skies over Sevastopol, on 7 November (the anniversary of the communist Revolution) a pair of MiG-3s downed a Ju 88 directly over the main naval base in full view of hundreds of Sevastopol's citizens. Seventeen days later the Soviets made a multi-wave strike on enemy airfields in Saki and Sarabuz in the Crimean steppe. Of the five participating MiG-3s one was lost to flak.

No serviceable MiG-3s were available in the Crimea in December 1941 to support ground forces at Kerch and Feodosiya, and there were none available to patrol Sevastopol's airspace either. But in the last few days of the year two ships, the *Bialystok* and the *Nogin*, delivered repair kits and several overhauled AM-35A engines to make many unserviceable MiGs airworthy once again. In early January 1942 7th IAP's 2nd Squadron, commanded by Capt Dmitry A Kudymov, also arrived at the Cape of Chersonese to provide some badly needed reinforcements.

Together with other fighter types, the MiGs patrolled over Sevastopol and occasionally flew ground attack missions. During this time the Soviet command considered German long-range artillery positions to be priority targets because of the round-the-clock shelling of the city. In April the

Black Sea Fleet Air Force pilots study a map before a combat sortie during the defence of Sevastopol

enemy moved the headquarters of VIII *Fliegerkorps* to the Crimea, and there was a corresponding increase in Luftwaffe activity. Now bombing raids on Soviet airfields were added to the intensive shelling.

The details of the death of Black Sea Fleet Air Force CO Gen Nikolay Ostryakov and the Deputy Head of the Naval Air Force Gen Fedor Korobkov, are well known to Soviet historians. They were killed on 24 April 1942 when six Ju 88s made a surprise attack on aircraft repair workshops at Kruglaya Bay. In that single raid the defenders of Sevastopol lost not only two senior commanders and their accompanying staff, but also three aircraft sheds with valuable equipment and a large stock of parts and supplies. A MiG-3 in the process of repair was also destroyed.

Ostryakov's successor, Gen Vasiliy Ermachenkov, immediately formed 3rd OAG, commanded by Col G G Dzyuba. The unit's inspector of operations, Capt K

MiG-3 '5', flown by Capt K D Denisov, CO of the 7th IAP, Black Sea Fleet Air Force, taxies out at the start of yet another defensive patrol over Sevastopol in early 1942

D Denisov, reported the availability of between 98 and 115 serviceable combat aircraft. The final report before the fall of Sevastopol indicated that the group's complement of aircraft had declined to 64, but a notable drop in the number of serviceable fighters had been apparent in May. By this time the remaining MiG-3s had been allocated to the 6th GIAP, and all would be captured by the enemy because they lacked the range to escape to the Caucasus in July.

From March onwards the Germans had systematically attacked key Soviet sea ports and bombed and torpedoed Soviet shipping in the Black Sea. The theatre commander, Vice Adm F S Oktyabrsky, reported to Adm Kuznetsov on 2 April that there had been an increase in Luftwaffe activity. Oktyabrsky also explained that the tonnage of available cargo vessels had been reduced by a quarter over the previous two months, with enemy aircraft making 28 attacks on ships and 56 strikes on naval installations. A minelayer, a tanker, two barges, two patrol craft and a large cargo vessel had been lost.

On the very day that Oktyabrsky was making his gloomy report another large Soviet tanker was sunk by the Germans. The *Kuybyshev* was sailing from Novorossiysk to Kamysh-Burun, and it was lost despite being accompanied by a destroyer, two patrol craft and an aerial escort of MiG-3s. One of the pilots involved, Capt V S Chernopaschenko of 7th IAP, sacrificed his life by deliberately crashing into an attacking aircraft. Despite the heroic efforts of the escorting pilots, a torpedo struck the tanker at 1859 hrs. There was a massive explosion, and the Soviets were deprived of 4000 tons of fuel and oil. Eight seamen were killed.

With the enemy now attacking by day as well as by night, fighter pilots of the Black Sea Fleet had to be on patrol around the clock. But the MiG-3 was not considered well-suited to the role by air force commanders, who criticised its inadequate armament. One report analysing the previous ten months of operations judged that 'The most effective fighter types for night operations against German bombers were the Yak-1s and I-16 cannon-armed aircraft. They had enough firepower and speed to approach enemy aircraft and fire a lethal burst before the target had time to leave the area illuminated by search-lights'.

Another document, dated April 1942, reported on the losses sustained by the Black Sea Fleet Air Force. In ten months it had lost 33 MiG-3s, 14 of which had been shot down by the Germans, five were posted missing and one had fallen to flak. Eleven MiG-3s crashed on landing or taking off, and two more were destroyed by retreating Soviet troops.

In mid-summer 1942 MiG-3 pilots were defending the naval base at Novorossiysk. In a surprise attack on 2 July, the Germans sunk the flagship *Tashkent*. It was the start of a series of intensive raids against which the Black Sea Fleet Air Force could deploy 70 to 75 fighters of all types. Its reports indicate that ten to twelve MiG-3s were on continuous patrol to provide air cover for ships both in harbour and at sea and to intercept raiding aircraft. Yet failures to detect incoming raids in time prevented these efforts from being effective.

On 8 July Capt Konstantin Denisov succeeded Lt Col Aleksey Dushin in command of 7th IAP at a time when the regiment possessed only 19 fighters of four different types – 7th IAP had nine of the fifteen MiG-3s then assigned to the Black Sea Fleet Air Force. Of these

This naval MiG-3 has had its underwing bomb racks removed. Note also that the propeller spinner has been painted in the squadron colours – probably yellow or blue

fighters, seven were completely worn out, and there were no spare parts. Veterans would recall how the regiment's chief engineer, N I Demenkov, worked a miracle in early August when, by cannibalising one of the MiGs for spares, he managed to restore all the others to a serviceable condition. But it was clear that using one fighter to repair the others represented a solution of limited applicability. There is, however, no documentary evidence to back up the story of the chief engineer's initiative.

In addition to the 39 MiG-3 fighters transferred to the Black Sea Fleet Air Force in the second half of 1941, 15 more would eventually arrive by July 1942. 7th IAP would be down to its last seven MiG-3s by 22 December, and only one of these was serviceable. The VVS RKKA had a total of 248 combat-ready MiG-3s, with a further 82 in need of repair. As the year wore on other frontline and air defence fighter units equipped with MiGs reported similar problems.

7th IAP struggled on nevertheless, and according to reports from the RUS-2 radar station in the Tuapse base air defence region, 7th IAP pilots flew MiG-3 sorties during April 1943. The improved early warning system helped guide Soviet pilots onto high-flying intruders, although attackers approaching at lower levels usually remained undetected.

The MiG-3s flown by 7th IAP in the spring of 1943 had been transferred into the Black Sea Fleet Air Force by the VVS RKKA and the inland Air Defence Forces. A total of ten aircraft had been overhauled and fitted with engines that possessed relatively long service lives. These combat-ready machines were well looked after by 7th IAP, which had significant experience of operating and maintaining the type by 1943.

The unit undertook an intensive training programme during the late spring and early summer. Acknowledged aces like K Nikonov, A Tomashevsky and B Abarin coached newly-arrived flying school graduates in flying the MiG-3 and in combat tactics. These intensive courses included target practice, aerobatics and mock air combat. In early July, however, deputy squadron commander Snr Lt Nikonov was killed in an accident. Subsequent investigation discovered that he had made a violent pull-out from a dive, and that this had resulted in a large area of skinning being torn from the wing. The fighter had stalled and plunged to the ground. The pilot had failed to open his cockpit canopy.

MiG-3s remained in frontline service with the Black Sea Fleet Air Force's 7th IAP well into 1943

Future Yak-9 ace Vladimir Voronov joined 7th IAP in May 1943 from a naval flying school. He recalled participating in a series of mock battles between MiG-3s and P-40 Kittyhawks which were also in service with the regiment – both types had their supporters among the unit's pilots. While the US-built fighter demonstrated superior horizontal manoeuvrability and had better armament and equipment, the MiG-3 beat it in vertical manoeuvres. Statistics showed that the MiG-3 usually came out on top.

At that time 7th IAP's MiG-3s were performing a variety of tasks. Amongst the most challenging assignments were the night exercises with anti-aircraft searchlight batteries. They tested pilots' instrument flying skills, while the searchlight crews had to practice following fast-moving small targets. By that time the main naval base had been moved to Poti, where the exercises were often flown during a period of moonless nights. Pilots had to operate using their instruments, positioning their aircraft against the dimly-lit shoreline. They were unable to test their nocturnal expertise in combat, however, due to a decline in German aerial activity.

THE BALTIC THEATRE

The introduction of the MiG-3 to the Baltic theatre had been planned to happen earlier than in the Black Sea. Indeed, in February 1941 the Red Banner Baltic Fleet Air Force was ordered to re-equip the 3rd Squadron of 5th IAP, commanded by Hero of the Soviet Union Maj Petr Kondratev, with the aircraft. This was followed in April by an order for the 1st Squadron to follow suit, and for both to complete their conversion and be combat-ready by 1 July. When the new equipment failed to arrive the pilots' study was confined to theory.

13th IAP followed 5th, and well-known I-16/La-5 ace Vasiliy Golubev, who served in the former regiment before the war, later described the preparations for the arrival of the first MiGs;

'The most unpleasant were the days of ground training. Every day from breakfast until lunch and then until dinner late in the afternoon, we sat under canvas tents which grew hotter and hotter under the summer sun. All day long we were busy diligently copying complicated fuel and oil pipeline layouts, and even the intricate hydraulics of the MiG-3 landing gear, into our workbooks. There were thousands of figures, and we had to learn them all off by heart – propeller diameter, wingspan, fuselage length, main wheel track, fin height. And after that instrument layout and readings, speed modes, dozens of failure warnings available to the pilot and many other things.'

All these classroom studies proved futile. 13th IAP would never receive any MiG-3s and 5th IAP began its flying training much later than planned. According to archive documents, only six MiG-1s and seven MiG-3s had been accepted by 5th IAP by 22 June. They were allocated to the squadrons led by Capts Azevich and Umansky, but neither unit had combat-trained pilots. Meanwhile, 25 MiG-3s of the variant with underwing machine guns (designated MiG-3bk by the Fleet Air Force) were assembled and earmarked for Lt Col V S Koreshkov's 71st IAP.

Another notable Baltic ace, Igor Kaberov, witnessed the first fatal accident involving an MiG-3 at the Baltic Fleet's Nizino airfield. It happened during a training exercise soon after the outbreak of the war when the MiG-3, flown by a pilot named Obozny, collided with an I-16 piloted by Lt Khripunov. Both were 5th IAP pilots and both lacked radio. A warning signal rocket was fired too late to prevent the accident.

The first MiG-3 combat sorties were reported to have been flown in late June, and they involved interceptions of enemy reconnaissance aircraft. The situation in the Baltic theatre deteriorated rapidly, and soon Baltic Fleet Air Force units were forced to throw whatever they had into halting the advancing German ground troops. On 10 and 11 July there were reports of MiGs escorting SB medium and DB-3 long-range bombers attacking enemy troops near Porkhov. By the end of the month the MiG-3s were also being used as ground-attack aircraft.

During July the Baltic Fleet Air Force was subsumed into the Northern Front Air Force, commanded by Gen A A Novikov, in an attempt to improve operational planning. A Baltic Fleet Air Force staff report of the period noted that 'The most suitable fighter aircraft types for the purposes of making strikes on enemy ground troops proved to be the I-16 and the I-153. They had sufficient firepower (when equipped with rocket projectiles) and demonstrated greater survivability than the newer LaGG-3, MiG-3 or Yak-1. The latter could often be brought down or forced to land with a single bullet or splinter puncture of the engine cooling system'.

Taking such considerations into account, the MiG-3s were initially employed rather sparingly in this role. Yet by 19 April 1942, 24 had been lost, many during ground-attack missions. That same day a large number of Soviet aircraft had been destroyed on the ground in a surprise attack on Nizino airfield by Bf 110s of ZG 26 – 24 fighters, including six MiG-3s, were left in flames.

Wearing flying helmets, Snr Lt Igor Kaberov (Hero of the Soviet Union with eight individual and 18 shared victories, mostly claimed in the La-5) and regimental deputy CO Capt Aleksander Myasnikov were amongst the most experienced MiG-3 pilots in 5th IAP, Red-Banner Baltic Fleet Air Force

Capt Aleksander Myasnikov, who took part in the Winter War against Finland in 1939/40, was killed in combat on 11 September 1942, having completed 315 operational sorties during which he had claimed 18 personal and shared victories

An appendix to the *Red Banner Baltic Fleet Air Force in the Great Patriotic War* describes four ramming attacks by MiG-3 pilots in 1941. All those involved – Capt Ivan Gorbachev and Snr Lts Dmitry Zosimov, Nikolay Mitin and Mikhail Martyschenko – survived. Indeed, the latter was to be the most successful MiG-3 pilot in the theatre. Having qualified on the new fighter in late July, he claimed four victories and another shared by November. Martyschenko's final tally was 18 victories by war's end. Published personal files indicate that all four men were experienced fighter pilots, but there is no confirmation of their success in any German reports. Gorbachev's ramming attack on a Messerschmitt on 14 September remains unacknowledged, and German sources state that all aircraft returned safely to their airfield at Osel island. At the time, however, the most intensive air combats were reported to have been fought over the archipelago of Moonsund. Soviet pilots emerged from a prolonged battle to claim the destruction of 48 enemy aircraft.

Existing documentation indicates that the so-called Baltic Fleet Air Force Osel Air Group, which was formed on 9 September under the command of Maj A A Denisov, had a strength of six MiG-3s, of which five were serviceable. On the 13th one of the fighters was lost to German naval anti-aircraft fire west of the island of Saaremaa. It was the only loss reported by the Osel Air Group during the defensive operations, and the pilot was able to bail out. However, on the return flight to Kogula, a serious accident resulted in the loss of another MiG-3, which crashed at Bychye Pole airfield. Three days later Snr Lt Kasatkin's element shot down a Bf 109E of JG 54's training flight to open the score for the unit's MiG pilots.

There is a widespread belief, supported by Soviet historical studies and the recollections of those involved, that 5th IAP's participation in the defence of Kronstadt between 21 and 27 September 1941 was not only heroic but also highly effective. This belief is based on an overestimation of the part played by the pilots of LaGG-3s, Yaks-1 and I-16s in preventing the Luftwaffe from disabling the Baltic Fleet. While the enemy did indeed fail to accomplish its goal of destroying the Soviet warships, both German and Russian studies have indicated that Soviet fighter pilots did not achieve the success in the theatre that has been claimed for them.

Small groups of five to eight Soviet fighters patrolled the area at low to medium altitude to avoid being shot down by coastal anti-aircraft batteries or warships. While the Messerschmitts did not provide regular escorts for German level and dive-bombers, they were never far away. Usually, Jagdwaffe fighter pilots would head for Kronstadt in advance of the bombers, flying at high altitudes to engage the Soviet fighters. Surprise attacks were frequently effective, and even Soviet sources acknowledged the 13-to-2 loss ratio in the Luftwaffe's favour. For the Soviets the most disappointing outcome was their fighter pilots' failure to shoot down any of the enemy bombers.

By the end of September the Baltic Fleet Air Force had received reinforcements in the form of 31 new MiG-3s. In the first month of fighting the Soviets lost 13 MiGs, 20 in the second and 13 more in the third. From then on combat activities became less intense and the losses declined. Indeed, in the final four months of 1941 the Baltic Fleet

Air Force reported the loss of just three more MiG-3s. 71st IAP had been hardest hit in 1941, losing ten MiG-3s.

The siege of Leningrad posed acute difficulties in providing enough food to keep the city's population from starving. Attempts to organise supply channels over Lake Ladoga or by air were met by stiff opposition from the Germans. Then, in September, the Leningrad Front command undertook the most important organisational step

This 61st Fighter Air Brigade MiG-3 was damaged by enemy fire, but its pilot managed to make a belly landing

by forming a combined air group comprising VVS RKKA and naval fighter squadrons. Its sole purpose was to provide air cover for the 'road of life' over the lake. While some Soviet fighter pilots provided cover for these lifelines, others like the MiG-3-equipped 12th Independent Red Banner Squadron mounted patrols over the ports and other crucial facilities east of Lake Ladoga. By early 1942, the unit, commanded by Maj V A Rozhdestvensky, was equipped with two MiG-1s, 11 MiG-3s and seven LaGG-3s.

Despite the pilots' good training and the high serviceability of the fighters, most of the interception missions proved futile. At that time the enemy preferred to attack in small elements of two or four Bf 109s, which declined to engage in disadvantageous conditions and escaped at full throttle. Nevertheless, in one engagement in early 1942 four MiG-3s encountered four Bf 109Fs. Snr Lt N P Khromov shot one down, which, according to German data, was operated by I./JG 54. It crashed into the sea off Kobona.

The Germans had their revenge on 6 February when a flight of MiGs and five other fighters, patrolling the Lake Ladoga route between Zhikharevo and Voybokalo, were bounced by Bf 109s. A MiG-3 of the 12th Independent Fighter Air Squadron (*Otdelnaya Istrebitenlaya Aviaeskadrilya*, OIAE) was shot down, its pilot surviving by taking to his parachute. His wingman attempted to escape but he unfortunately

Armourers gained access to the MiG-3's machine gun magazines via doors behind the engine. They have been removed from this naval aircraft to allow the magazine to be reloaded

flew into the Soviet anti-aircraft zone and was shot down. Although wounded, the pilot bailed out and was taken to hospital upon landing. Leningrad Front Air Force chief engineer A V Ageev wrote in his diary;

'6 February 1942 – MiG-3 4828 was shot down right over front staff headquarters in Gorky village and crashed near Pegaylo. That fighter was piloted by my brother, Konstantin. His MiG caught fire at once and his arm was broken by a splinter, but he somehow managed

to bail out. While he was descending in his parachute, the German pilot tried to shoot him but one of the I-16 pilots prevented that vulture from doing so.

'7 February 1942 – I have just visited Konstantin at Field Hospital No 979. He had lost a lot of blood and needed a transfusion, which he received in time. Despite severe pains and burns, my brother did not faint and kept a stiff upper lip.'

The Soviet pilots' heroic performance in protecting the vital supply route across the lake was acknowledged in a report by the Ladoga Fleet Executive Officer. This states that between 21 May and 30 September the convoys had transported, in either direction, 650,204 people, including civilians, evacuated 24,654 wounded personnel and delivered 705,882 tons of cargo. The report concluded with the hopeful statement that 'Convoys continue to shuttle across Lake Ladoga'.

German efforts to win dominance of Lake Ladoga included assembling about 40 various craft in preparation for an operation to capture Sukho Island. If this was achieved communications between Leningrad and the mainland would become even more difficult. Soviet sailors and airmen inflicted serious losses on the Germans, however, forcing them to withdraw and leave the area on 22 October 1942.

Within 24 hours the Baltic naval and attached frontline aviators had flown 111 combat sorties, including 62 attacks on retreating enemy vessels. Attacking in four waves of 12 aircraft, the MiG-3s were equipped with AO-25 and AO-15 light splinter bombs carried in underwing racks. This was probably the only case of fighters of that type being used to attack enemy ships. It might be suggested that of the four barges claimed by the 12th OIAE, only one was in fact sunk and another set on fire before they escaped. Poor weather conditions aided the Germans in their escape, and all the MiG-3s got away undamaged too.

12th OIAE operated MiG fighters until May 1943 when it was finally re-equipped with Yak-7Bs. The eight surviving MiG-3s were then transferred to the 3rd Training Air Regiment of the Baltic Fleet Air Force, while its two MiG-1s were employed as target towing aircraft. By the end of 1943 all the surviving MiGs had been transferred to the Pacific Fleet Air Force.

THE NORTH SEA

MiG-3s were rare birds in the North Sea Fleet Air Force. On 16 July 1941 ten new aircraft and their crews were transferred from the Black Sea theatre, and they would remain the only examples of the type to operate with the North Sea Fleet Air Force. All ten fighters were flown by 72nd SAP, commanded by Hero of the Soviet Union Maj Georgiy Gubanov. The MiG-3s' main functions in the North Sea theatre included protection of the base area and flying interception missions.

The first MiG-3 victory confirmed by enemy sources came on 19 July. when Lt Zakhar Sorokin shot down a Bf 110C of 1.(Z)/JG 77. Both crew members were taken prisoner. Two days later 72nd SAP also reported its first documented losses when MiG-3 3497, piloted by Lt Kalugin, was caught in the blast of an exploding bomb while taking off, causing it to nose over. The fighter was damaged beyond repair and the pilot severely wounded and hospitalised. His wingman, Ayrapetyan,

This MiG-3 of 72nd SAP, Northern Fleet Air Force is about to be loaded with the crated bombs seen here lashed to a reindeer-powered skid

was posted missing, together with his MiG-3 3492, after taking off. It was assumed that he had been shot down by German fighters.

The most effective performance by 72nd IAP's fighter pilots came on 9 August when they intercepted enemy aircraft raiding the port of Vayenga. Soviet pilots claimed to have shot down six Ju 88s, although I./KG 30 acknowledged losing only Wk-Nrs. 3468, 3351 and 3454. One crashed in Soviet territory and the other two were written-off after making emergency landings at their bases. Five MiG-3s were among the 18 Soviet fighters that took off to counter the raid. Snr Lt D I Sokolov was flying one of these machines, and he claimed an escorting Messerschmitt destroyed. This was probably Bf 109E Wk-Nr. 3363, the loss of which was admitted by the Germans. Soviet losses amounted to two I-153 *Chaikas* shot down and one DB-3F bomber destroyed on the ground. Four other bombers were damaged.

Some attempts were made in the Baltic theatre to use MiG-3s to attack airfields, but the idea was abandoned following the loss of two fighters on 22 August. Three MiG-3s had made a dive-bombing attack on the airfield at Khebukten, dropping six FAB-50 light bombs from an altitude of 5000 m (16,250 ft). The fighters then flew straight through the enemy anti-aircraft fire zone, and the MiG-3 flown by Tolstikov was damaged and eventually written off after an emergency landing near Cape Set-Navolok. The other MiG-3 hit the sea and sank in Kola Bay, killing its pilot, Lt Schevchenko.

The last MiG-3 loss reported by 72nd IAP in 1941 was dated 25 October, the North Sea Fleet Air Force staff reporting that Lt Zakhar Sorokin had had to make a forced landing in the tundra due to engine failure. His situation was aggravated by radio failure and the lack of skis or emergency rations. It took him six days to make his way back to his base, suffering from frost-bite. Sorokin subsequently lost both feet and spent 14 months in hospital before his determination enabled him to recover and return to active combat service as a fighter pilot.

Having claimed 11 individual aerial victories, Sorokin was awarded the title of Hero of the Soviet Union on 19 August 1944. As far as is known, five of those kills were scored while he was flying the MiG-3 (two Bf 110s, two Ju 88s and one Bf 109), thus making him the most successful ace on the type in this theatre. However, the widely-publicised story of

MiG-3 pilot Jr Lt Lt Verkhovtsev of 72nd SAP, Northern Fleet Air Force

A MiG-3 from 61st Fighter Air Brigade, Red Banner Baltic Fleet Air Force is refuelled from a GAZ-AA bowser truck

Sorokin ramming a Bf 110 during the fierce battle of 25 October 1941, and his subsequent duel with the German crew on the snowy landscape, was obviously a piece of propagandistic fiction because there are no documents to support the story.

North Sea Fleet Air Force MiG-3 losses for 1942 totalled just one aircraft. On 19 July a pilot called Sokolov brought his holed and burning fighter back to base. He was able to save his life but not his aircraft, which was completely burned out. In the second half of the year the MiG-3 fleet stood idle for much of the time for want of spare parts. In April 1943 the last three MiG-3s were redeployed to the Baltic Fleet Air Force. On 12 July they were passed to 12th OIAE and operated by that unit until spring 1944.

The table below lists the number of MiG-3s that were serviceable and unserviceable in Soviet Fleet Air Force units during the first 18 months of the war;

Fleet	10/7/41	1/10/41	5/12/41	1/5/42	18/11/42
North Sea	1/3	3/2	2/2	1/3	-/3
Baltic Sea	46/8	13/1	13/2	6/5	7/4
Black Sea	4/5	20/7	11/3	12/10	4/3
Total	51/16	36/10	26/7	19/18	11/10

Archive documents state that after the first two years of the Great Patriotic War – the most crucial period – combat losses in all fleets totalled 95 MiG-3s. This figure included 61 shot down by enemy aircraft, five lost to anti-aircraft fire (including one to 'friendly' fire), 16 posted missing from combat sorties and 13 MiGs destroyed on the ground. Non-combat losses amounted to 38 MiGs, including 11 in crash-landings, 26 in non-operational flying accidents and one destroyed by retreating Soviet troops. Five more MiG-3s were written off due to

A MiG-3 of 7th IAP, Black Sea Fleet Air Force returns to an airfield near Sevastopol following a patrol in 1942

being completely worn out. Total losses of the Fleet Air Forces amounted to 138 MiG-3s.

Early in the third year of the war the VVS RKKA's last two frontline MiG-3 fighters were transferred to the Fleet Air Forces from the reserve and allocated to 7th IAP. As at 1 November 1943 the Black Sea Fleet Air Force had on its strength 26 serviceable MiGs, with four more reported as having been transferred from flying schools to 7th IAP. That left 12 remaining in the 3rd Naval Flying School. The largest group of MiGs was now in the Pacific theatre, where the Pacific Fleet Air Force had 55 MiG-3s, with nine others attached to the North Pacific Flotilla Air Force.

THE FAR EAST

The first MiG-3s were shipped to the Far East before the outbreak of the Great Patriotic War. By 22 June 17 had been delivered to the Pacific Fleet Air Force's 6th IAP, based at Uglovaya railway station, near Vladivostok. Early in 1942 a decision was taken to deploy 40 MiG-3s to the Japanese frontier because of the uneasy situation there. When they finally arrived in July, most went to 6th IAP, although some were also sent to 31st and 39th IAPs based at Olga Bay and Vladimir Bay, respectively. Organisationally, these units were part of the Vladimir/Olga Flotilla Air Force.

Despite the inevitable accidental losses, strength of the Pacific Air Force fighter arm steadily increased as new shipments arrived. By late 1944 it had 83 MiG-3s, operated by 6th, 31st and 39th IAPs, while the North Pacific Flotilla Air Force's 41st IAP had 12. Most were combat-ready. By comparison, of the 16 MiGs remaining in the Black Sea theatre at this time, only four were fully serviceable. This discrepancy in numbers can be explained by the fact that the Far Eastern Navy received 'new old' fighters during the first quarter of 1944, while the naval aviation units in the west had by then begun to write them off one by one.

An example was MiG-3 3338. It joined the Baltic Sea Fleet Air Force's 7th IAP in 1943 from a regular frontline wing. In March 1944 it was transferred to the Pacific Fleet Air Force and on 25 July 1944 it was written off. The following day another MiG-3, 4855, with a similar history was also written off. Both fighters had undergone five or six overhauls by then, and their ultimate fate was typical. None would survive until the start of Soviet military action in the Far East. By the time the short war with Japan began in August 1945 all the MiGs had been written off.

So ended the era of the MiG-1 and the MiG-3. They had joined the Soviet armoury at a critical time, and although they were often found inferior to the fighters they opposed, it was not always because of defects in the design produced by Mikoyan and Gurevich. They were high altitude fighters called upon to fight at low and medium altitudes. Many of their failings were the result of manufacturing faults, inadequate pilot training and inflexible tactical doctrine.

For a time the MiGs represented the Soviets' most modern fighters, and as such they made a major contribution to the defence of the Motherland. In the skies over Moscow in particular, MiG-3 pilots performed heroically at a time when the Red Army inflicted upon the hitherto invincible German Wehrmacht its first defeat.

APPENDICES

APPENDIX 1

Most successful MiG-3 aces

No	Rank and Name	Unit(s)	MiG-3 Victories	Total Victories	Comments
1	Snr Lt A A Dmitriyev	15th IAP	15 individual + 2 shared	15+2	Killed 13/11/41
2	Snr Lt I D Chulkov*	41st IAP	11+1	11+1	Killed 3/2/42
3	Snr Lt E M Ryzhikov*	BSF AA, 32nd, 7th IAPs	10+3	11+5	-
4	Lt I N Zabolotny*	16th IAP	10+0	10+0	Killed 4/1/42
5	Lt S V Makarov*	180th IAP	9+9	10+13	Killed 10/2/42
6	Maj K A Gruzdev	402nd IAP	9+4	9+6	-
7	Lt I F Golubin*	16th IAP	9+2	13+2	Killed 1/11/42
8	Snr Lt K E Seliverstov*	55th IAP	9+2	9+2	Killed 15/10/41
9	Snr Lt N A Kozlov*	162nd, 439th IAPs	9+1	16+6	-
10	Jr Lt V A Figichev*	55th IAP	9+0	15+2	-
11	Snr Lt A A Lipilin*	41st IAP	8+3	8+5	Flew 135 MiG-3 sorties
12	Lt S F Dolgushin*	180th IAP	8+2	17+11	-
13	Snr Lt A F Kovachevich*	27th IAP	8+1	19+5	-

Notes

* Hero of the Soviet Union

– Dates of death given only for pilots killed while flying a sortie in the MiG-3

APPENDIX 2

Pilots who scored five or more victories flying MiG-3s

No	Rank and Name	Unit	MiG-3 Victories	Total Victories	Comments
1	Snr Lt I P Shumilov*	16th IAP	7+2	16+2	-
2	Capt P N Dargis	7th, 19th, 565th IAPs	7+6	7+6	-
3	Capt V A Kiselyov	34th IAP	7+4	7+4	-
4	Snr Political Instructor N P Baskov	445th IAP	7+2	9+2	-
5	Lt A G Lukyanov*	34th, 487th IAPs	7+2	8+5	-
6	Capt V D Rozhkov	445th, 177th IAPs	7+2	7+2	-
7	Capt N A Aleksandrov	34th IAP	7+1	7+1	Flew 101 MiG-3 sorties
8	Capt G V Zimin*	42nd IAP	7+1	14+4	-
9	Snr Lt K F Ivachev	55th IAP	7+0	7+0	Killed 14/10/41
10	Snr Lt D.G. Korovchenko	41st IAP	7+0	12(?)+(?)	-
11	Snr Lt P A Tikhomirov	41st IAP	7+0	8(?)+(?)	-
12	Snr Lt A I Nikitin	7th, 19th, 153rd IAPs	6+7	13+5	-
13	Lt S A Rubtsov	120th IAP	6+6	9+6	-
14	Snr Lt A N Storozhakov*	154th IAP	6+6	6+6	Killed 10/9/41 during 153rd sortie

No	Rank and Name	Unit	MiG-3 Victories	Total Victories	Comments
15	Snr Lt N A Semenov	16th IAP	6+4	7+4	-
16	Snr Lt A G Shevtsov	180th IAP	6+3	13+7	-
17	Snr Lt M P Barsov	124th IAP	6+2	6+2	Killed 8/8/42 during 101st sortie
18	Snr Political Instructor A V Rudenko	23rd, 28th IAPs	6+2	11+2	-
19	Capt N T Kitayev	25th IAP	6+1	24+5	-
20	Snr Political Instructor A M Sokolov*	129th IAP	6+1	8+1	-
21	Capt N P Baulin	402nd IAP	6+0	6+0	Killed 2/10/41 in crash during test-flight
22	Snr Lt N I Vlasov*	42nd IAP	6+0	10+0	-
23	Lt V M Gvozdev	402nd IAP	6+0	7+2	-
24	Snr Lt P T Tarasov*	15th IAP	6+0	30+3	-
25	Snr Lt G V Gromov*	147th IAP	5+13	7+17	-
26	Snr Lt V F Korobov	34th IAP	5+8	9+8	Flew 414 MiG-3 combat sorties
27	Snr Lt A G Kubyshkin	401st IAP	5+6	5+6	Flew 70 MiG-3 combat sorties
28	Snr Lt S D Baykov	34th IAP	5+4	5+6	-
29	Capt M V Kuznetsov*	15th IAP	5+3	21+6	-
30	Snr Lt A D Pechenevsky	177th IAP	5+3	5+3	-
31	Lt I Z Tyapin	177th IAP	5+3	5+3	-
32	Capt F S Chuykin	27th IAP	5+3	11+6	-
33	Capt A N Katrich*	27th IAP	5+2	5+7	-
34	Snr Lt M F Mitrofanov*	445th IAP	5+2	20+3	-
35	Capt N P Gorodnichev*	129th IAP	5+1	14(?)+(?)	-
36	Jr Lt S G Ridny*	126th IAP	5+1	21(?)+(?)	-
37	Lt V I Skryabin	25th IAP	5+1	11+3	-
38	Lt M D Baranov*	183rd IAP	5+0	24+0	-
39	Capt F F Golubnichy	263rd IAP	5+0	12+3	-
40	Lt K A Kryukov	120th IAP, 12th GIAP	5+0	21+10	-
41	Capt D I Ledovsky	34, 487th IAPs	5+0	5+0	-
42	Lt P Y Likholetov*	159th IAP	5+0	23+7	-
43	Maj K N Orlov	4th IAP	5+0	5+0	-
44	Capt P A Pilyutov*	154th IAP	5+0	14+1	-
45	Snr Lt A I Pokryshkin*	55th IAP	5+0	53+6	-
46	Snr Lt Z A Sorokin*	NSF AA, 72nd SAP	5+0	10+0	-

Notes

* Hero of the Soviet Union
– Dates of death given only for pilots killed while flying sorties in the MiG-3

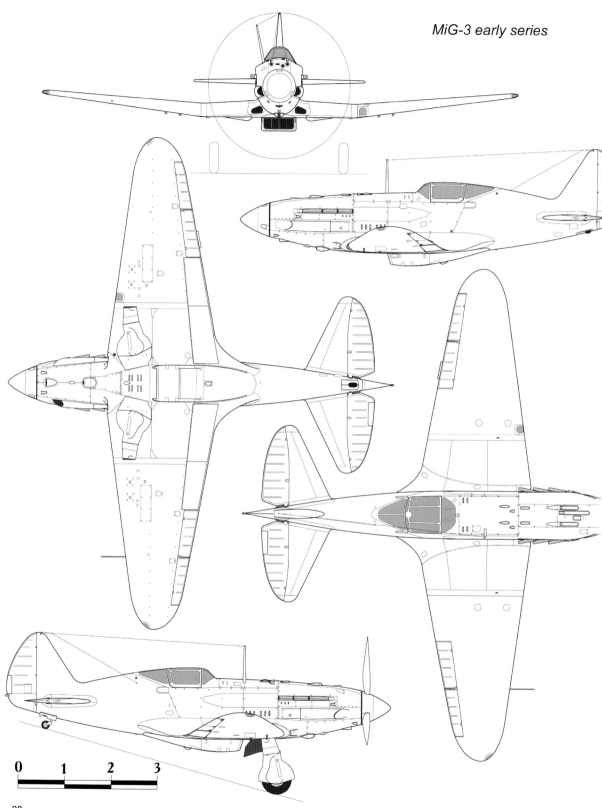

MiG-3 early series

0   1   2   3

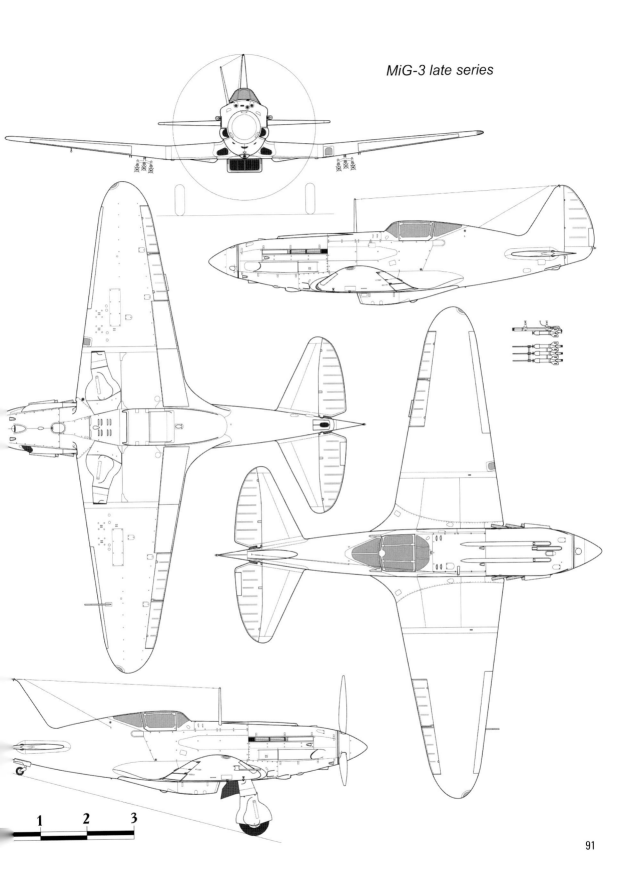

MiG-3 late series

1

MiG-3 of Snr Lt Sergey Baikov, 34th IAP, 6th IAK, Moscow region, August 1941

Before the war Snr Lt Baikov had been known for his skill as a pilot, particularly in bad weather. He scored his first victory on 27 October 1941 while flying a MiG-3 with 6th IAK of the Air Defence Forces, Baikov being one of several pilots who shared in the destruction of a Bf 110 that crashed near the town of Naro-Fominsk in the Moscow region. Between then and 5 December, when the Soviets launched their counter-offensive near the capital, Baikov claimed three more victories. He ended the war flying Yak-9s with 12th GIAP of the 1st Fighter Air Army of the Air Defence Forces.

2

MiG-3 of Capt Viktor Kozulya, 38th Reconnaissance Squadron, Western Front Air Force, Moscow region, August 1941

Prewar, Viktor Kozulya was better known as a test parachutist than as a pilot, and his achievements were recognised by the award of the Order of Lenin. Kozulya made his first jump in May 1932, and by February 1938 he had 378 to his credit. This total included 70 test jumps and 28 water landings. Later that year Kozulya joined the NII VVS of the VVS RKKA, where he was a parachute instructor. When the air force began forming special units manned by test pilots, he became a member of the 38th Squadron, qualified on the MiG-3 and led a reconnaissance unit equipped with fighters that had been modified to carry special cameras. It was while flying a MiG-3 on 18 August 1941 that Kozulya was shot down and taken prisoner. He spent 42 months in PoW camps before being repatriated, and he continued his testing career after the war. Post-war, Viktor Kozulya became the holder of Soviet and world parachuting records.

3

MiG-3 of Snr Lt Aleksey Kubyshkin, 401st Special Purpose IAP, Western Front Air Force, Smolensk region, July 1941

Aleksey Kubyshkin had been a test pilot at the NII VVS of the VVS RKKA from late 1934. By the time war with Germany broke out in June 1941, Kubyshkin was a qualified MiG-3 pilot involved in the conversion training of 28th IAP near Lvov. He became one of the highest scoring pilots of 401st Special Purpose IAP, which was formed at the end of June 1941 by Lt Col Stepan Suprun and manned by test pilots. Kubyshkin claimed five and six shared victories over German aircraft and fought in 32 aerial battles, all while flying MiG-3s. According to official records, he was an exceptional combat pilot who was also particularly skilled in aerobatics. All told, he flew a total of 70 combat sorties. After the war Aleksey Kubyshkin continued test flying, and he was one of the first Soviet pilots to fly a jet. Eventually completing 8500+ flights, he tested more than 130 different aircraft types, and was highly decorated. Indeed, Kubyshkin received two Orders of the Red Banner, two Orders of the Patriotic War and an Order of the Red Star for his combat exploits with the MiG-3 in June-July 1941.

4

MiG-3 3660 of Jr Lt Ivan Golubin, 16th IAP, 6th IAK, Moscow region, December 1941

This fighter had been written off in a landing accident and was found on a dump by regimental engineer A Markov, who ordered technician Shustov to take the aircraft to Lyubertsy and try to repair it. The work was completed in 13 days, Golubin test flying it and then using 3660 on operations. He achieved his first aerial victory on 24 October 1941 when he shot down a Ju 87 near the village of Kamenskoe. Golubin emerged from the fierce fighting around Moscow as the highest-scoring of the capital's defenders, with nine and two shared victories to his name (all of them claimed while at the controls of a MiG-3). He received the title of Hero of the Soviet Union on 4 March 1942, but was killed during a ferry flight on 1 November that same year.

5

MiG-3 of Maj Pavel Putivko, 31st IAP, 8th IAD, Northwestern Front Air Force, Kaunas region, June 1941

Delivered to 31st IAP in April 1941, this aircraft was flown by the regimental CO, Maj Pavel Putivko, from the 18th of that month onwards. Together with other MiG-3s, the fighter was damaged in an early Luftwaffe air raid on the regimental airfield and captured by the advancing Wehrmacht following the occupation of Kaunas. Putivko was wounded during one of his first combat sorties of the war while flying another aircraft.

6

MiG-3 of 172nd IAP, 6th IAK, Moscow region, 23 February 1942

This fighter, displaying the slogan 'For the Party of the Bolsheviks', was assembled by the workers of Moscow's Factory No 1 using parts that had been left behind when the rest of the plant was evacuated to the east. Other popular slogans included 'For Stalin' and 'For the Motherland'. The fighter depicted was delivered to 172nd IAP of 6th IAK on the Western Front in a formal ceremony on 23 February 1942. It is not known who flew the fighter for the first time, but it was soon transferred to 122nd IAP. This unit was based at Vnukovo airfield near Moscow and directly subordinated to the commander of the Front Air Force, Gen S A Khudyakov. According to the recollections of veterans, Lt Viktor Bashkirov flew the fighter on two occasions. Bashkirov, who shot down three Messerschmitts in August 1942, was to become one of the highest scoring aces of 122nd and 519th IAPs with 14 and two shared victories. Most of his kills were achieved while flying Yak fighters, and he was later awarded the title of Hero of the Soviet Union.

7

MiG-3 of 180th IAP, 46th IAD, Kalinin Front Air Force, Kalinin region, October 1941

This aircraft was captured by German troops in the Kalinin area in October 1941. It had almost certainly been assigned to 180th IAP of 46th IAD. The Wehrmacht not only captured several MiG fighters but also the regimental CO, A P Sergeev, who was immediately executed.

8
MiG-3 of 120th IAP, 6th IAK, Moscow region, March 1942
This aircraft was photographed during an official ceremony when 120th IAP, commanded by Lt Col A S Pisarenko, formally received the Guards banner presented to the unit. From 8 March 1942 the regiment was designated 12th GIAP.

9
MiG-3 of Capt Ivan Dolzhenko, 15th IAP, Northwestern Front Air Force, Kaunas region, June 1941
Based at Kaunas, Potsunai and Vencai airfields, 15th IAP received MiG-3s on the eve of war. This fighter was flown by battalion commissar P S Leshchenko, but it was squadron CO Capt Dolzhenko who was at the controls on 22 June when German bombers were intercepted. Dolzhenko shot down a Ju 88, but he was killed a few hours later whilst flying his seventh sortie of the war's first day.

10
MiG-3 of Lt Ivan Shults, 15th IAP, Northwestern Front Air Force, Kaunas region, June 1941
Lt Shults, a 25-year-old pilot with two years' flying experience, was a deputy squadron navigating officer within 15th IAP. He saw action from the early hours of 22 June, and claimed to have shot down three German aircraft. The fighter assigned to Shults became unserviceable following his first combat mission, so he switched to the MiG-3 depicted here. Shults failed to return from his second sortie, his body subsequently being recovered and buried near Kaunas.

11
MiG-1 of 126th IAP, 9th IAD, Western Front Air Force, Belostok region, June 1941
126th IAP was one of the first regiments to receive the MiG-1 prewar. The unit was originally based at Belsk airfield, but it moved to Dolubovo, 18 km (11 miles) from the border, soon after the arrival of its MiGs. Here, pilots continued their conversion training onto the MiG-1/3, and by the outbreak of war 68 of the regiment's 103 pilots had completed the course. A series of raids by Bf 109s and Bf 110s created chaos at Dolubovo, and it is not known which of the regiment's pilots flew this MiG-3 prior to it being captured virtually intact by Wehrmacht troops on the evening of 22 June 1941.

12
MiG-3 of Maj Yakov Titaev, 148th IAP, Southwestern Front Air Force, Kharkov region, May 1942
Displaying the message 'For Stalin', this aircraft was flown during the spring of 1942 by 148th IAP's navigation officer, Maj Titaev. He was one of the regiment's most successful pilots, scoring three aerial victories in the MiG-3. On 11 May 1942 he was due to meet the CO of the Southwestern Front Air Force, Gen F Ya Falaleev, but he had to fly a sortie that same day as an escort for Pe-2s raiding Kharkov airfield. Titaev failed to return and was posted missing. It is possible that he had fallen victim to either Oberfeldwebel Reinhold Schmetzer or Wilhelm Baumgartner of II./JG 77

13
MiG-3 of Capt Ivan Rybin, 148th IAP, Southwestern Front Air Force, Kharkov region, June 1942
This fighter, which displays an unusual 'spotted' camouflage scheme, was one of ten MiG-3s still operated by 148th IAP in May 1942. On 3 June Capt Rybin used it to intercept a German reconnaissance Do 215, which he duly shot down – this was the third aerial victory he had achieved while flying the MiG-3. Eight days later the regiment was ordered to transfer its remaining seven MiG-3s to 101st IAD of the Air Defence Forces, after which MiGs were no longer operated by frontline units of the VVS RKKA. Rybin, now a major, was killed in an combat over Kuban on 26 April 1943. By then he had eight and five shared aerial victories to his credit. Rybin was posthumously awarded the title of Hero of the Soviet Union.

14
MiG-3 of Snr Lt Aleksander Lipilin, 41st IAP, 6th IAK, Moscow region, August 1941
Flown by Aleksander Lipilin, this fighter was involved in the battle for Moscow between June and mid-August 1941, when it was used to intercept German bombing raids and reconnaissance missions. 41st IAP continued to see combat on the northwestern front until October 1941, when it was committed to the next phase of the battle for Moscow. According to official records, by the end of January 1942 Lipilin had flown 128 combat sorties, during which he had scored five and three shared victories in three different MiGs. He had also destroyed numerous targets on the ground. Lipilin was duly awarded the title of Hero of the Soviet Union on 24 February 1942.

15
MiG-3 of Snr Lt Mikhail Nekrasov, 148th IAP, Southwestern Air Force, Kiev region, September 1941
Mikhail Nekrasov was flying an I-153 on 28 June 1941 when he claimed an He 111 destroyed. When 148th IAP converted to the MiG-3 a short while later, Nekrasov was one of the few pilots in the regiment to have combat experience. According to the records, Nekrasov claimed a Ju 88 on 25 September and an 'He 113' (probably a Bf 109F) on 2 October. By the time of his death in August 1943, now Lt Col Nekrasov had accumulated a score of 12 victories, a tally which included eight Bf 109s.

16
MiG-3 of Lt Aleksey Nikitin, 7th IAP, Leningrad Front Air Force, Leningrad region, October 1941
Lt Nkitin saw combat during the Soviet-Finnish conflict, and by the end of July 1941 he had been credited with three (two Ju 88s and a Bf 109E) and one shared (Ju 88) aerial victories. That August he added three more to his score, with another two in September. Nikitin subsequently flew the P-39 Airacobra, and by the end of the war his score had reached 13 and five shared victories achieved during a total of 200 combat sorties. On 10 February 1943 Nikitin received the title of Hero of the Soviet Union, and in the latter stages of the war he served as safety inspector of his air division and then of his air army. Nikitin died in a flying accident on 20 September 1954, aged 36.

17

MiG-3 of Regimental Political Instructor Anatoliy Rudenko, 28th IAP, Northwestern Front Air Force, Demyansk region, October 1941

This aircraft was transferred from a reserve air regiment to 28th IAP, where it was flown by regimental political instructor Anatoliy Rudenko. He claimed his first success on the second day of the war in the east when he shot down an Hs 126. Rudenko added two more victories to his score in July 1941. His MiG-3 was damaged during a combat sortie in October, but Rudenko managed to force-land in neutral territory and make his way back to Soviet lines. Rudenko's tally had risen to 11 and two shared victories by war's end. He had also been promoted to the rank of lieutenant colonel.

18

MiG-3 of Jr Lt Anatoliy Lukyanov, 34th IAP, 6th IAK, Moscow region, August 1941

Following tests at the NII VVS and a change of engine, this white-tailed MiG-3 was transferred to the Moscow Air Defence Forces in June 1941. Jr Lt Lukyanov flew the fighter on the night of 22 July 1941 in response to the first German nocturnal raid on Moscow. He succeeded in shooting down one of the attackers near Borovsk, and the following evening Lukyanov encountered another bomber in the sky over Moscow. This time, although he opened fire on it, his MiG-3 was hit by Soviet flak and the intruder escaped. Lukyanov subsequently shot down a further six German aircraft (and shared in the destruction of two more) while flying the MiG-3, earning him the title of Hero of the Soviet Union.

19

MiG-3 of Lt Viktor A Kiselev, 34th IAP, 6th IAK, Moscow region, August 1941

This 34th IAP MiG-3 has been equipped with additional underwing fuel tanks so as to increase its endurance when on patrol west of Moscow. The fighter is also armed with UBS 12.7 mm machine guns in place of the more common ShKAS weapons of the same calibre. On the night of 10 August Viktor Kiselev used this aircraft to ram an He 111 whose crew was later taken prisoner. In the wake of this attack Kiselev became the first regimental pilot to receive the Order of Lenin. In September 1942 Snr Lt Kiselev was flying a cannon-armed MiG-3 when he shot down two German bombers. Later, he participated in the service tests of the ultimately unsuccessful MiG-9 fighter, which was a standard MiG-3 airframe fitted with an M-82 radial engine.

20

MiG-3 2171 of Lt N M Essin, 5th IAP, Red-Banner Baltic Fleet Air Force, Finland, July 1941

Essin was an experienced fighter pilot who had already been awarded the Order of the Red Banner for his participation in the war with Finland. On 12 July 1941 his fighter was hit by Finnish anti-aircraft fire and following a forced-landing he was taken prisoner – he died whilst a PoW on 28 February 1942. Essin's damaged MiG-3 was inspected by a group of Finnish pilots headed by Capt A Hassinen of LLv 14, a unit which was then equipped with Gloster Gladiators. Although the Finns did not attempt to restore Essin's crashed fighter, they ordered 20 captured MiG-3s from the Germans and planned to equip one squadron with them. The order was accepted and the captured aircraft were disassembled, crated and loaded onto a ship, but all were destroyed by fire following a Soviet air raid on the port of Danzig (others reports say Stettin) in December 1942. In March 1943 the Germans delivered the first batch of 20 Bf 109Gs to Finland, so the matter of supplying further captured MiG-3s did not arise again.

21

MiG-3 of Lt Ivan Dubovik, 7th IAP, Northern Front Air Force, Karelia, July 1941

Dubovik claimed his first success on 22 July 1941 when he shot down an enemy aircraft near the Finnish airfield of Utti. He fought in a further 44 aerial battles and took his score to 12 and nine shared victories, although only one of these was claimed in a MiG-3. Despite these achievements Dubovik did not receive the title of Hero of the Soviet Union. He was flying Yak-9s when the war ended.

22

MiG-3 of Snr Lt Aleksander Shevarev, 31st IAP, Northwestern Front Air Force, Kaunas region, June 1941

Shevarev opened his combat score on 9 July 1941 when he shared in the destruction of a Bf 110, and on 7 August he shot down a Ju 88 near Idritsa. By the end of the war, now Maj Shevarev had a score of 13 and one shared victories to his name. He received the title of Hero of the Russian Federation on 11 October 1995 – 50 years after the end of the war.

23

MiG-3 of Capt K D Denisov, 7th IAP, Black Sea Fleet Air Force, Tuapse region, August 1942

Denisov was one of a group of aviators to become acquainted with the MiG-3 when Soviet test pilot Stepan Suprun demonstrated aerobatic flying in the new fighter to 8th IAP personnel in March 1941 at the Kacha flying school. However, when war broke out Denisov was flying the I-16 and then, from March 1942, the Yak-1, and he scored most of his combat victories in these two fighter types. Denisov converted to the MiG-3 in June 1942, and on 23 October he received the title of Hero of the Soviet Union for achieving seven and six shared victories. 7th IAP distinguished itself during the defence of the Caucasus when it was mostly equipped with MiG-3s. Maj Denisov, flying a P-40, achieved his most notable success on the evening of 22 April 1943 when he shot down an He 111 near Poti. The German bomber was piloted by the CO of 7./KG 27, Oberleutnant Erich Thiel (a holder of the Knight's Cross).

24

MiG-3 of Capt S N Polyakov, 7th IAP, Leningrad Front Air Force, Leningrad region, September 1941

A 7th IAP squadron commander, Polyakov was a Muscovite who participated in the defence of Leningrad. After 5th IAD was reinforced by a regiment of ground-attack aircraft, Polyakov decided to convert to the Il-2. Soon appointed CO of 174th Attack Air Regiment, he had flown a total of 42 combat sorties by the time of his death in action on 24 December 1941. Polykov perished at the controls of a U-2 liaison biplane when he strayed into a German air raid whilst flying from Cape Kapitolovo to Kasimovo. He was posthumously awarded the title of Hero of the Soviet Union.

25
MiG-3 of Capt Aleksander A Sharmin, 7th IAP, Black Sea Fleet Air Force, Kuban region, May 1943

A squadron commander, Sharmin had several MiGs in his unit, and they were probably the only such fighters in the fleet to participate in the defence of Novorossiysk. They were also used to perform reconnaissance flights over the mountain passes in the Caucasus. By the time Soviet and German forces fought for control of the Kuban region in the spring of 1943, the regiment had only two MiG-3s left on its strength. Aleksander Sharmin became known not only for his combat score but also for his ability to keep MiG-3s flying, despite a shortage of spares parts and worn-out engines.

26
MiG-3 of Capt Konstantin Nikonov, 7th IAP, Black Sea Fleet Air Force, Caucasus region, July 1943

After 7th IAP had accepted 15 surplus MiG-3s from Moscow Air Defence Forces, Capt Nikonov was involved in ferrying them to the Caucasus for the conversion training of new pilots. During a mock air battle on 6 July 1943 his aircraft crashed near Mikha-Tskhakaya airfield, in the Caucasus. Subsequent investigation revealed that due to the high humidity of the Kolkhida valley in summer, the plywood skin of the wing had delaminated, leading to the accident. Nikonov was an experienced fighter pilot with some 800 flying hours to his credit. Already the holder of the Order of the Red Banner, he was awarded his second decoration posthumously.

27
MiG-3 of Snr Lt Kuzma Seliverstov, 55th IAP, Southern Front Air Force, Beltsy region, June 1941

During the first two weeks of the war Lt Seliverstov was a flight commander serving in the same regiment as well-known ace Aleksander Pokryshkin. One of the first MiG-3 aces, he claimed nine and two shared victories. This success saw Seliverstov nominated for the title of Hero of the Soviet Union on 6 August 1941, by which time he had flown 132 combat sorties. Seliverstov, flying his 170th sortie, was killed in combat with four Bf 109s near Rostov on 15 October 1941. He was credited with downing two of his opponents prior to his own demise. Note that Seliverstov's MiG-3 boasts two underwing guns.

28
MiG-3 of Jr Lt Grigoriy Gorban, 185th IAP, 6th IAK, Moscow region, March 1942

This fighter displays an overall white winter camouflage scheme. Lt Gorban claimed his first victories in the spring of 1942, being credited with one and nine shared destroyed. By war's end his score had reached ten and 14 shared kills, claimed during the course of 371 combat missions.

29
MiG-3 of Jr Lt Grigoriy German, 42nd IAP, Western Front Air Force, Moscow region, August 1941

This fighter has been adorned with the slogan 'For the Motherland'. German, who flew the MiG-3 from the very start of the war, shot down two Hs 126 reconnaissance aircraft on 16 August 1941 followed by a Ju 88 three days later. He received the title of Hero of the Soviet Union on 28 September 1943, by which time he had taken his score to 17 and one shared victories – most of these kills were claimed in Yak-1s.

30
MiG-3 of Lt Mikhail Baranov, 183rd IAP, Western Front Air Force, Moscow region, December 1941

Mikhail Baranov joined 183rd IAP in September 1941 and shot down two Bf 109s that same month. By the end of the year his tally had reached six enemy aircraft destroyed, five of which he had scored while flying the MiG-3. During the fierce fighting in the Stalingrad area in July and August 1942 Baranov claimed 13 more victories, although his unit had long since swapped its MiG-3s for Yak-1s. Baranov was awarded the title of Hero of the Soviet Union on 12 August 1942. By the time of his death in a crash on 15 January 1943 his score had reached 24 enemy aircraft destroyed.

31
MiG-3 Capt Ivan Zabolotny, 16th IAP, 6th IAK, Moscow region, February 1942

This aircraft, bearing the slogan 'For Stalin!', was flown by 16th IAP squadron commander Capt Ivan Zabolotny. In the period from mid October to mid December 1941 he shot down nine German aircraft, five of which were Ju 88s. On 4 January 1942 Zabolotny destroyed a sixth Junkers bomber, although he was fatally wounded by the Ju 88's return fire in the process. 16th IAP's ranking MiG-3 ace, Zabolotny was posthumously awarded the title of Hero of the Soviet Union on 27 June 1942.

32
MiG-3 of Lt Ivan Kholodov, 28th IAP, 6th IAK, Moscow region, February 1942

A 28th IAP flight commander, Kholodov had initially seen combat during the Soviet-Finnish 'Winter War' of 1939-40. At the start of the war with Germany he was serving with 23rd IAP, and he shared in the destruction of a Bf 110 heavy fighter. After his transfer to 28th IAP, Kholodov was able to raise his score to six victories by the end of 1941. In March 1942 he was awarded the title of Hero of the Soviet Union. By war's end, having been promoted to the rank of lieutenant colonel and made CO of 111th GIAP, Kholodov had 14 and six shared victories to his credit.

INDEX

References-illustrations are shown in **bold**. Plates are prefixed pl, with captions on the page in (brackets).

Abarin, Snr Lt B 79
Achkasov, Lt S V **68**
Ageyev, Snr Lt Konstantin 83-4
Akimov, Jr Lt 12
Aksyutin, Lt 12
Aleksandrov, Capt N A 88

Alekseenko, V I 11
Avdeev, Lt Mikhail 74
Azevich, Capt 81

Bagdasaryan, Maj 33
Baranov, Lt Mikhail D pl**57**(95), 89
Baranov, Snr Lt A A 42
Barsov, Snr Lt Mikhail P **62**, 89
Bashkirov, Lt Victor **24**, 92

Baskov, Snr Political Instructor N P 88
Baulin, Capt N P 89
Baykalov, Jr Lt M K 59
Baykov, Snr Lt Sergey pl**50**(92), D 89
Belousov, Lt T G **67**
Blagoveshchenskiy, Col V G 39
Bocharov, Lt I I 68
Bogorodetsky, Lt Col A K 33
Bolovlenkov, Capt V B 34

Boyarshinov, Capt N 23
Brunov, Anatoly 9

Cherkasov, Lt Col 24
Chernopaschenko, Capt V S 78
Chesnokov, Lt A 34
Chulkov, Snr Lt I D 19, 48, 48-9, 88
Churinov, Capt V A 43
Chuykin, Capt F S 89

Dargis, Capt P N 88
Demidov, Maj Gen A A 15, 25, 32, 65
Demidov, Maj N F 33, 69
Denisenko, Lt A 68
Denisov , Capt Konstantin D pl**55**(94), 77-8, **78**, 79
Denisov, Maj A A 82
Didenko, Capt G V 39
Dmitriev, Lt A A 23, 43, 44, 45, 46, 88
Dobzhenko, Capt I AS 23
Dodonchenko, Lt 42
Dolgushin, Lt Sergey F 73, 88
Dolzhenko, Capt Ivan pl**52**(93)
Dovgiy, Jr Lt V I 64, 68
Dubovik, Lt Ivan pl**55**(94)
Durnaykin, Lt Z A 68
Dushin, Lt Col Aleksey 79

Ekatov, Arkady 9, 11
Erchenko, Jr Lt N F 18
Eremeev, Snr Lt P V 59
Essin, Lt N M pl**54**(94)
Evstigneev, Lt 39
Evstratov, Sgt 64
Evtushenko , Jr Lt 12
Evtyukhin, Capt V Y 43

Farafonov, Capt O M 27, 36
Fedorov, Snr Lt Aleksander E **69**, 69, **70**
Feklyunin, Lt 64
Figichev, Jr Lt V I 15, 88
Frimerman, Jr Lt 48

Gallay, Capt Mark **cover**(4) 19-20
German, Jr Lt Grigoriy pl**57**(95)
Gladyshev, Snr Lt 24
Golitsin, Maj G M 41-2
Golubev, Snr Lt Vasiliy 80-1
Golubin, Lt Ivan F pl**50**(92), 66, 67, 88
Golubnichy, Capt F F 89
Gorbachev, Capt Ivan 82
Gorban, Jr Lt Grigoriy pl**56**(95)
Gorbatyuk, Snr Lt Evgeny 11, 69
Gorgalyuk, Lt Aleksander 30
Gorodnichev, Capt N P 89
Gorshkov, Maj D M 66
Gorshunov, Capt 43
Grigorenko, Snr Lt **20**
Gromov, Snr Lt G V 89
Grunin, Jr Lt N L 63-4
Gruzdev, Maj F A 43, 88
Gubanov, Maj Georgiy 84
Gurevich, Mikhail **7**, 7, 8
Gvozdev, Lt V M 89

Ivachev, Snr Lt K F 37, 88
Ivanchenko, Lt Grigoriy **61**
Ivanov, Col V P 25, 37

Jungman, Snr Lt K I 36

Kaberov, Snr Lt Igor **81**, 81
Kalarsh, Maj D L 12
Kalugin, Lt 84
Kamenshchikov, Lt Vladimir G 58-9
Karmanov, Capt Afanasy 26, 26-7
Karpenko, Maj G P 66
Kasatkin, Snr Lt 82
Katrich, Capt Aleksey N 63, 89
Khlusovich, Capt I M 72
Kholodov, Lt Col Ivan M 33-4, pl**57**(95), 69
Khomyakov, Maj V I 20
Khripunov, Lt 81
Khromov, Snr Lt N P 83
Kiselev, Capt Viktor A **63**, 63, pl**54**(94), 88
Kitayev, Capt N T 89
Klimov, Col I D 12, 61

Kokkinaki, Lt Col Konstantin 20
Kokorev, Jr Lt D V 18
Kondratev, Maj Petr 80
Koreshkov, Lt Col V S 81
Korobov, Snr Lt V F 89
Korolev, Maj M I 64
Korovchenko, Snr Lt D G 19, 48, 88
Kovachevich, Snr Lt A F 88
Kozlov, Snr Lt N A 88
Kozulya, Capt Viktor pl**50**(92)
Kruglov, Capt 61-2
Krupenin, Capt I V 11
Kryuchkov, Jr Lt 68
Kryukov, Capt K A **68**, 89
Kudymov, Capt Dmitry A 77
Kuldin, Lt Col L G 11
Kutakhov, Lt P S 43
Kuzmichev, Snr Lt I G 48, 49
Kuznetsov, Capt M V 43, 89

Ledovsky, Capt D I 89
Likholetov, Lt Petr Y 41, 89
Lipilin, Snr Lt Aleksander A 19, 48, 49, pl**53**(93), 88
Lukin, Jr Lt Vasiliy 41
Lukyanov, Jr Lt Anatoliy G 12, 59, pl**54**(94), 88
Lyubimov, Capt Ivan 74

Makarov, Lt Sergey V 72-3, 88
Malov, Jr Lt V V 36
Martyschenko, Snr Lt Mikhail 82
MiG-3: '5' **78**, 78; No 2171 pl**54**(94); No 3338 87; No 3492 85; No 3497 84; No 3660 pl**50**(92)
Mikoyan, Artyom **7**, 7, 8, 9
Mikulin, Alkeksander 6
Mitin, Snr Lt Nikolay 82
Mitrofanov, Snr Lt M F 89
Monastyrsky, Lt G F 24-5
Murashko, Jr Lt A M 24
Muravyev, Jr Lt 65
Musienko, Lt N A 44
Myasnikov, Capt Aleksander **81**, **82**

Naydenko, V M 12
Nekrasov, Snr Lt Mikhail pl**53**(93)
Nemtsevich, Lt Col Yuri 58
Nikanorov, Lt G I 44
Nikitin, Snr Lt Aleksey I pl**53**(93), 88
Nikolaev, Col A P 29
Nikonov, Capt Konstantin pl**56**(95), 79
Novikov-Ilyin, Capt V V 72

Oborin, Snr Lt K P 27
Obozny, Jr Lt 81
Orlov, Capt Konstantin N 27, 36, 89
Orlov, Maj Vladimir 26, 36
Orlov, Snr Lt F A 29
Orlyakhin, Lt Col S I 70
Ovechkin, Capt B V 23

Panov, Capt Aleksey 30
Pasechnik, Snr Lt I S 72
Pashko, Lt I N 44
Pavlov, Maj N Z 74
Pechenevsky, Snr Lt A D 89
Petrov, Lt V F 33
Pilyutov, Capt P A 39, 89
Pirozhkov, Jr Lt B G 64
Pisarenko, Lt Col A S 93
Platov, Lt Col S I **64**
Podpryatov, Lt A P 34
Pokryshkin, Snr Lt Aleksander I 14, 36-7, **37**, 89
Polikarpov I-200 prototype **7**, 7-9, **8**, 9, 10, **13**, 13
Polikarpov, Nikolay **6**, 6
Polupanov, Snr Lt 24
Polyakov, Capt S N pl**55**(94-5)
Popov, Lt 49
Pronin, Maj Aleksander **61**, 61-2, **62**
Proshakov, Snr Lt Afanasy 21
Putivko, Maj Pavel I 22-3, pl**51**(92)
Puzeykin, Maj V V 29

Rabkin, I G 9-10
Radugin, Jr Lt A A 18
Reshetnikov, Lt K D 42
Reznik, Lt Col 19
Ridny, Jr Lt S G 58, 89

Rozhdestvensky, Maj V A 83
Rozhkov, Capt V D 88
Rubanov, Lt 64
Rubtsov, Lt S A 88
Rudenko, Snr Political Instructor A V 33, pl**54**(94), 89
Ryabchy, Commissar 21
Ryazanov, Jr Lt Aleksey 34
Rybin, Capt Ivan pl**53**(93)
Rybkin, Col L G 11, 12, **59**, 59, 67
Ryzhikov, Snr Lt Evgraph 75, 77, 88

Samodurov, Snr Lt 65
Savva, Lt N I 77
Scherbina, Jr Lt N G 12, 59
Schevchenko, Lt 85
Schultz, Lt I I 23
Schurov, Lt Vasiliy 41
Seliverstov, Snr Lt Kuzma E 37, pl**56**(95), 88
Semenov, Capt Aleksander F 29, 72
Semenov, Snr Lt N A 89
Sentemov, Capt S E 71
Sergeev, Capt A P 72, 93
Shagov, Lt 29-30
Sharmin, Capt Aleksander A pl**56**(5)
Shemyakov, Snr Lt A D 23
Shevarev, Snr Lt Aleksander pl**55**(94)
Shevtsov, Lt Aleksander G 41, 89
Shinkarenko, Col Fedor I 65, 72
Shults, Lt Ivan pl**52**(93)
Shumilov, Lt Ivan P 66, 67
Shumilov, Snr Lt I P 88
Sinev, Maj 41-2
Skornyakov, Capt S A 48
Skryabin, Lt V I 89
Smirnov, A V 12
Smyslov, Lt S S 23
Sobolev, Lt V 34
Sokolov, Lt Col D I 85, 86
Sokolov, Snr Political Instructor A M 17, 89
Sorokin, Lt Zakhar A 84, 85-6, 89
Startsev, Jr Lt G N 64
Stefanovsky, Lt Col Petr M 13-14, 19, 60-1, 70
Storozhakov, Snr Lt Aleksey N 40, 45, 88
Strokachenko, Jr Lt V I 43
Stuchkin, Lt N N 68
Suprun, Lt Col Stepan R 19, 20

Talalikhin, Jr Lt Viktor **65**
Tarasov, Snr Lt P T 23, 89
Telegin, Lt P 75
Tikhomirov, Snr Lt P A 19, 48, 88
Timofeev, Maj S I 72
Timokhin, Lt N B 24
Titaev, Maj Yakov pl**52**(93)
Titarenko, Lt Dmitry S **38**, 39
Tkachenko, Maj Andrey 38-9
Tolstikov, Lt 85
Tomashevsky, Snr Lt A 79
Tomilin, Snr Lt V M 88
Toropchin, Col N S 44-5
Trunov, Capt M G 12, 59
Tsisarenko, Snr Lt Nikolay **61**, **62**
Turenko, Col Evgeny G 41, 47
Tyapin, Lt I Z 89

Varenik, Technician **15**
Vasin, Snr Lt A E 43
Verkhovtsev, Jr Lt **85**
Verov, Commissar F F **38**
Vinokurov, Capt A M 68
Vlasov, Lt Col N I 65, 89
Voronin, Maj I A 41
Voronov, Jr Lt Vladimir 80

Yershov, Lt Col V S 47

Zabelin, Snr Lt P I 19, 48
Zabolotny, Lt Ivan N pl**57**(95), 66-7, 68, 88
Zanin, Lt Dmitriy **61**
Zavgorodny, Lt 66
Zaytsev, Lt V M 36
Zelenov, Lt P T 43
Zharin, Jr Lt A M 27
Zimin, Capt G V 71, 88
Zosimov, Snr Lt Dmitry 82